Praise for *On the*

Thoughtful, helpful, insightful, *On the Shoulders of Hobbits* reminds us just how much is to be gained by standing on the shoulders of Tolkien and Lewis, those Christian literary giants.

　　—MICHAEL WARD, Oxford Centre for Christian Apologetics and co-editor of *The Cambridge Companion to C. S. Lewis*

Louis Markos has written a helpful guide to the moral and spiritual realities embodied in J. R. R. Tolkien's hobbit tales and C. S. Lewis' Narnian novels. Here he probes the darkness of evil, the perils of pilgrimage, the terror and gift of death, as well as the summons to shape our lives according to all seven of the virtues: discernment and justice, courage and temperance, hope and faith and love. In so doing, he recovers a Christian humanism for an age that remains largely blind and deaf to the sacred drama of God's mysterious work in the world.

　　—RALPH C. WOOD
　　　University Professor of Theology and Literature
　　　Baylor University

The mistake that Uncle Andrew made was not that he believed wealth could be brought back from Narnia. His mistake was in refusing to bring back the right kind of wealth—it is wisdom we need, not more steel and battleships. Louis Markos has remedied that problem, importing a great deal of wisdom from Narnia, and Middle Earth as well, with plenty to spare. I am happy to recommend *On the Shoulders of Hobbits*.

　　—DOUGLAS WILSON, author of *What I Learned in Narnia*

Louis Markos' thoughtful exploration of virtue through the writings of J. R. R. Tolkien and C. S. Lewis is a valuable resource for parents, teachers, and young people seeking models and guides for living a life shaped by, and infused with, the richness of Christian virtues.

—HOLLY ORDWAY, Houston Baptist University and author of *Not God's Type*

A book that richly celebrates the place of story in our lives—even as it invites us to walk the road with, and glean life lessons from, some of J. R. R. Tolkien's finest characters.

—KEVIN BELMONTE, editor of *A Year with G. K. Chesterton*, and lead historical consultant for the film *Amazing Grace*

ON THE
SHOULDERS
H*of*OBBITS

the Road *to* Virtue *with*
Tolkien *and* Lewis

LOUIS MARKOS

MOODY PUBLISHERS
CHICAGO

Edited by Christopher Reese
Interior design: Smartt Guys design
Cover design: Brand Navigation, LLC

Cover Image: Steve Gardner/PixelWorks/istock
Author Photo: Michael Tims
Houston Baptist University

Library of Congress Cataloging-in-Publication Data

Markos, Louis.
  On the shoulders of hobbits : the road to virtue with Tolkien and Lewis / Louis Markos.
    p. cm.
  Includes bibliographical references and index.
  ISBN 978-0-8024-4319-9
  1. Tolkien, J. R. R. (John Ronald Reuel), 1892-1973—Criticism and interpretation.
2. Lewis, C. S. (Clive Staples), 1898-1963—Criticism and interpretation. 3. Christianity and literature. I. Title.
PR6039.O32Z6936 2012
823'.912—dc23

                                              2012022461

For Alex and Stacey

For enjoying these tales with me

And allowing me to see them through new eyes

CONTENTS

FOREWORD

"Why should I read this book? What is it about?" That's the question you want a foreword to answer.

Well, this book is about life. Your life. It's not fantasy, it's realism. It's the so-called realistic books that are usually fantasy. When you close the covers of *The Lord of the Rings* or the Chronicles of Narnia, you intuitively know that you are not exiting an unreal world and entering a more real one, but exactly the opposite.

The best educational advice for life that I ever heard was my father's: "Just be sure you don't get all A's in your subjects but flunk life."

We humans are the only beings in the universe who can flunk life, because we have a free choice about what kind of life we will lead and what kind of human beings we will be, good or evil. We make these choices not, like angels, instantly and timelessly, but gradually, in each of our many big and little choices between good and evil throughout the drama that is our lifetime.

How do we become good or evil? When Plato asked in his *Meno* how human beings become good (virtuous), he suggested four ways: (1) by teaching ("knowledge is virtue"); (2) by practice (forming habits); (3) by nature (i.e., being born virtuous); (4) in some other way (i.e., against nature, by force). Most philosophers—Oriental as well as Western—give one of these four answers: Plato, #1; Confucius, #1 and #2; Aristotle, #2; Rousseau and Lao Tzu, #3; Hobbes and the "Realists," #4.

All these philosophers are wrong, probably because most of them do not have children. Parents and children know the answer: by example. By having moral heroes.

That's why reading great literature, next to meeting people, is the single most effective way to learn not to flunk life. Life is a story, and therefore moral education happens first and most powerfully through stories, e.g., through books.

The greatest book of the twentieth century, according to four different polls, is *The Lord of the Rings*. And the greatest children's stories ever written are the Chronicles of Narnia (I dogmatically assure you of that!).

On the Shoulders of Hobbits is the logical conclusion from all of the above facts. Read it. It will help you fall in love with these two great works, their heroes, and their values. It will baptize your imagination and fertilize the soil of your soul so that you become the kind of person who doesn't flunk life.

—Peter Kreeft
Boston College
July 2012

STORIES *to* STEER BY

There is little doubt that our lives are both freer and easier than those of our grandparents and great-grandparents. Science and technology have liberated us from much toil and increased our leisure time, while advances in medicine, education, transportation, and communication have multiplied our options and brought the world (quite literally) to our fingertips. Nevertheless, there is one way in which our lives have become less restful and more constricted than those of our ancestors. Although life today is easier, it is also far more complicated. As the number and type of decisions that we must make on a daily basis have increased severalfold, the fixed standards and universal truths to help guide us in our decision making have seemingly decreased to an even greater degree. At the very moment that we most desperately need moral, spiritual, and aesthetic touchstones, we find that our signposts have been knocked down, our boundaries shattered, and our verities exploded.

We are, in many ways, a civilization adrift on the stormy seas of relativism and existentialism. The first "ism" has robbed us of any transcendent standard against which we can measure our thoughts, our words, and our deeds; the second has emptied our lives of any higher meaning, purpose, or direction. Our compass is broken and the stars obliterated, and we are left with nothing to navigate by but a vague faith in the modern triad of progress, consumerism, and egalitarianism. They are not enough.

What do we need to get our ship back on course? First, we need a revived awareness of and respect for the traditions on which Western culture was built: namely, the Judeo-Christian and the Greco-Roman. The rigid secular humanism that dominates in our public schools and universities, in our courts, and in our media needs to give way to a distinctly *Christian* humanist vision. Such a vision seeks to affirm that we are free, rational creatures who possess innate dignity and whose lives and achievements are of intrinsic value (humanism), while acknowledging that we are fallen creatures in need of grace. It seeks further to embrace divine revelation as a check and a complement to human reason. Finally, it seeks to revive a clear sense that we live in a moral universe that is not only imbued with goodness, truth, and beauty, but in which the Good, the True, and the Beautiful are real and knowable things.

But even this is not enough. Though the restoration of theology and philosophy to their proper place is essential and primary, it needs to be accompanied by something else that will embody and incarnate it in the life of each individual citizen. For Western civilization has lost more than those laws, creeds, and doctrines on which it was built; it has lost as well the sacred drama that gave flesh and bone to those "naked" credal statements. We need the truth, but we also need to know how to live in and through and by that truth.

What we need, in short, are stories.

✵ ✵ ✵

Throughout most of the history of mankind, children have been taught good and evil, virtue and vice, honor and shame through the medium of stories: proverbs, parables, myths, legends, allegories, fables, etc. The great leaders who built fifth-century BC Athens (the cradle of humanism) were nurtured on tales from *The Iliad* and *The Odyssey* in the same way that the makers of Rome drank deeply from their vast reservoir of heroic tales about those who sacrificed all for their beloved republic. The true Christian is not just someone who believes certain things; he is someone who participates in a human-divine narrative: what many today refer to as a metanarrative or overarching story into which all of our individual stories can be grafted and from which they derive their ultimate meaning. To those who participate in them, these stories provide not only models of virtuous and vicious behavior but a sense of purpose—a sense that our lives and our choices are not arbitrary but that they are "going somewhere." They have, as Aristotle might say, a beginning, a middle, and an end. We live vicariously through the hero as he goes on his quest or fulfills his appointed mission, but we also seek to have the story played out in our own lives.

Bill Bennett—who with prophetic power warned us that the modern world has lost its moral compass—provided an invaluable service when he edited *The Book of Virtues*, a collection of sacred and secular tales from various cultures and historical periods that illustrate and embody the chief virtues that must be upheld and lived if civilization is to survive and thrive. Had he been born a century ago, Bennett would not have needed to write such a book; in the not so distant past, the stories were known and taught and cherished. Not so today. We have either forgotten the stories or refuse to allow ourselves to be shaped by them. Worse yet, we try to make up counter stories, politically correct fairy tales that are as paltry as the newfangled virtues they are meant to celebrate.

In our public schools today, there are only three virtues taught: tolerance, multiculturalism, and environmentalism. Really, there is only one: inclusivism or, better, egalitarianism—all people and ideas should be treated the same; all cultures are equally valid; man is not distinct from nature but merely another species. These modern "virtues" are not, in and of themselves, negative, but when they become the be-all and end-all of moral and ethical behavior, they become idols that blind us from our true nature and purpose. When all other virtues are reduced to a bland egalitarianism, our humanity is likewise reduced to a colorless, passionless, amoral existence. If we are to pull ourselves out of this lowest-common-denominator world, then we need a fresh infusion of story: one that will propel us back into the full romance of living. If our children are to successfully steer a course between the Scylla of standardless relativism and the Charybdis of purposeless existentialism, then they will need to be guided by transcendent truths embodied in universal stories.

Of course, in the past, stories were not only told for the entertainment and instruction of children; they performed that dual function for the adults as well. From the epics of Homer, Virgil,

Dante, and Milton to the verse romances, tales, and dramas of Spenser, Chaucer, and Shakespeare, premodern literature walked hand in hand with the art of storytelling. No hard and fast distinction was made between children's literature and adult literature, fairy tales and "serious" fiction; all drank from the same narrative well. The creating and telling of stories could be as much a vehicle of truth as science or math or philosophy.

This dual insight, that the split between fairy tales and serious fiction is a recent and artificial one and that stories can be powerful pointers to eternal truths, is not one that I came to on my own. I learned it from one of the twentieth century's most avid defenders of the premodern world: J. R. R. Tolkien. And I learned it not just from his critical essays, but from the great and timeless stories that he fashioned. Tolkien argued strongly and well (in his long essay "On Fairy-Stories") that a story that is only worth telling to children is not worth telling at all. He argued further that the only reason we consider romances and fairy tales to be childish fare is because the modern world has dismissed these genres as "old fashioned" and because old genres—like old furniture—eventually find their way to the nursery.

So he argued, and then, rather than leave that argument to hang untested in the abstract world of theory, he proved and incarnated it by almost single-handedly reviving the seemingly moribund genre of the fairy tale in the form of a deceptively simple children's story, *The Hobbit*. So greatly did *The Hobbit* delight adults and children hungry for the lost realm of fairy tales that they cried out for a sequel. In response, Tolkien spent the next decade and a half crafting a far richer and more mature work that would ratchet up its predecessor from a humble fairy tale to a full-scale epic in the tradition of *The Iliad*, *The Odyssey*, and

Beowulf. In this monumental work, *The Lord of the Rings*, written as a single epic novel but published in three installments due to the high price of post–World War II paper, Tolkien bequeathed to the world a new treasure trove of heroic tales and adventures with the power to reinvigorate classical and medieval virtues that our modern, technological age has deemed irrelevant. Together with *The Hobbit* and its prequel (*The Silmarillion*, which was published posthumously by one of Tolkien's sons), *The Lord of the Rings* stands as a lighthouse in a world that has not only lost its way, but has lost much of its virtue, its integrity, and its purpose.

This debt I owe to Tolkien, but I owe it as well to a friend of Tolkien who shared his love of enchantment, and who also sought, through critical essay and fantastic fiction alike, to restore stories to their proper place both as schools of virtue and repositories of truth. I refer, of course, to C. S. Lewis, whose beloved Chronicles of Narnia (1950–1956) appeared concurrently with *The Lord of the Rings* (1954–1956). While agreeing with Tolkien that the old genres needed reviving, Lewis argued further (in *A Preface to Paradise Lost*) that the modern distaste for and misunderstanding of the sacred and mythic narratives of the past is accompanied by an even stronger rejection of the old stock responses to virtue and vice that these narratives were meant to instill in us. And then, like Tolkien, he proved and incarnated this argument by spiriting his delighted audience away to his own magical world of talking animals and living trees where the old virtues and vices and the stock responses associated with them still existed.

Lewis's Narnia, like Tolkien's Middle-earth, is far more than a land of imagination; it is a place where honor and chivalry stand poised in mortal combat with the life-denying, faith-denying, hope-denying forces of evil. Though Lewis and Tolkien clad themselves, humbly and inconspicuously, in professorial robes, these two Oxford dons were in fact medieval knights come down from the past, heroes for a distinctly unheroic age.

❉ ❉ ❉

In imitation of these two knights, I shall attempt, in the chapters that follow, to revive a more traditional—and more transcendent—understanding of virtue and vice and of human purpose and dignity by catapulting the reader into the great and timeless stories bequeathed to us by Tolkien and Lewis. While my primary focus will be on Tolkien's tales of Middle-earth, I will close each of my chapters with a brief sojourn in Narnia. Though the fantasy worlds of Tolkien and Lewis are very different, and though Tolkien was not a fan of The Chronicles of Narnia, the fact remains that the two men shared the same premodern Christian understanding of good and evil, virtue and vice, beauty and ugliness. Indeed, I believe that the most effective way to draw out of *The Lord of the Rings* its golden treasures is by holding The Chronicles of Narnia beside it as a sort of literary philosopher's stone. Lewis was not only Tolkien's first great critic and advocate, he was a fellow traveler down the road of enchantment, and, as such, he is an invaluable guide to those who would follow in the footsteps of Bilbo and Frodo Baggins.

My approach throughout will be simple. Each chapter will take up a single theme-message-moral (the nature of goodness, the ill effects of greed, self-identity, etc.) that has been overlooked or dismissed by our age, and then that theme-message-moral will be illustrated and embodied in one or more episodes from *The Hobbit, The Lord of the Rings*, or *The Silmarillion*. I will then develop the theme further by zeroing in on a single passage from one of the seven Chronicles of Narnia that clarifies or complements Tolkien's message. In selecting these episodes, I will attempt to isolate areas that Tolkien and Lewis agreed on and (I believe) wished to convey to their modern readers. There were things that these two writers disagreed on, especially in terms of the scope and integrity of their created worlds; however, in this book, I will overlook those disagreements and focus only on those places where Tolkien and Lewis speak to us in what is nearly a single voice: a voice that carries within it the full weight of our Judeo-Christian, Greco-Roman past—not to mention the more "primitive" but no less noble legacy of the Norsemen and Anglo-Saxons.

In referencing *The Lord of the Rings*, I will give the book number (remember, *The Lord of the Rings* is not technically a trilogy but a single novel broken into six books), followed by the chapter number and the page number as it appears in the excellent one-volume edition first printed in Great Britain by HarperCollins Publishers in 1994 and reprinted in America by Houghton Mifflin Company. For The Chronicles of Narnia, I shall give the title of the individual novel, followed by the chapter number and the page number as it appears in the boxed-set edition published by Collier Books in 1970 (the edition that first carried me away as a child to the magic world of Narnia).

✳✳✳

The road lies plain before me, and I am eager to press on. However, before I begin, I would like to offer four brief caveats that will help clarify what exactly I will and will not be doing in this book.

First, although the message and diction of this book will be above the heads of children—though advanced teens should be able to follow the arguments—it is my hope that parents will read the chapters and then discuss the issues and episodes raised with their sons and daughters. Stories are meant to be shared, not read in isolation, and it is my hope that this book will initiate fruitful dialogue between parents and children and encourage them to enter as a family both into the adventures themselves and into the greater adventure of living, choosing, and yearning in a fallen world that is nevertheless filled with meaning, purpose, and beauty.

Second, I do not intend this to be a "scholarly" or "academic" work. Although I have provided, in an appendix, two bibliographical essays for those who wish to pursue further study or who wish to learn which books have most influenced my own reading of Tolkien and Lewis, I will not be referencing any secondary sources, nor will I be making use of footnotes. I want there to be nothing to distract us as we journey along the road from Middle-earth to Narnia. You might think of the chapters as a step-by-step series of interlocking meditations. Indeed, you may, if you wish, read them as you would a devotional: pausing to reflect on the "life-lesson" learned before moving on to the next. If you have children or grandchildren living with you, you might consider discussing one chapter per day with them, either during a meal or before they go to bed. Too often, "scholarly" books hold their subject at arm's length, adopting a detached and "objective" tone. The goal of this book is to enter, to embrace, to engage. Not to study but to learn from, not to judge but to be challenged by, not to analyze but to love.

Third, I will not be offering in this book a Christian or an allegorical or a symbolic reading of *The Lord of the Rings* or The Chronicles. I will not attempt to conform them to any single interpretative structure nor seek to trace all of the biblical, historical, or mythical allusions. Rather, I will mine them for insights into virtue as I would a rich vein of silver or gold. The main question I will ask is not what this or that character or event "means" or even what Tolkien or Lewis "intended" it to mean, but what we today, stranded as we are in the stormy seas of relativism and existentialism, can learn from the episodes that make up these two timeless works. I will be choosing, then, episodes that most effectively illustrate the particular theme being explored in that chapter, though in most cases it was the episodes themselves that first alerted me to the importance and urgency of the theme under discussion.

And that leads me, in turn, to my fourth and final caveat. Although I do not intend this book to be didactic or "preachy," it will be my goal in the following chapters to be both practical and convicting. I will be treating *The Lord of the Rings* and The Chronicles as wise and reliable sources of truth. Though I don't consider Tolkien or Lewis to be prophets in the biblical sense, I do believe that these deeply Christian authors allowed themselves to be conduits of the Good, the True, and the Beautiful. For both authors, stories were fun, but they were also serious business. Like Aslan, the Lion King of Narnia, they were to be loved and cherished but never trifled with. In the same spirit, though I mean for this book to be a fun, breézy, and energetic read, I do hope it will be attended to in a manner befitting its high seriousness. Our modern (and now postmodern) age has cast off—sometimes deliberately, but most often unthinkingly—many of the beliefs and virtues and disciplines that are necessary to the continuation of civilized life and the preservation of individual dignity and purpose.

As we travel the road with Bilbo and Frodo, it is my hope (if not my prayer) that we can revive those virtues and reawaken those stock responses that Tolkien and Lewis felt in their bones but which we and our society have allowed to fall to the wayside. I hope as well that as we journey down that road together, we will discover, as the hero of Bunyan's *Pilgrim's Progress* discovers, that God uses such journeys to strengthen our patience and our faith, to teach us to discern godly trials from demonic temptations, and to provide us with concrete models of heroism and villainy.

Let us begin.

PART ONE

The Road

the LURE *of the* ROAD

That life is a journey and that we are all travelers on the road is, at once, a well-worn cliché and a profound and universal truth. It lies at the heart of many of the greatest works of the human imagination (*The Odyssey*, *The Aeneid*, *The Divine Comedy*, *Canterbury Tales*, *Don Quixote*, *Pilgrim's Progress*, *Moby-Dick*, *Great Expectations*, *Huckleberry Finn*, *The Grapes of Wrath*, the Five Books of Moses, and the Acts of the Apostles), and it speaks to us at the deepest core of our being. No matter how comfortable our situation may be, no matter how permanent it may seem, we never quite feel at home. There is, in all of us, a vague restlessness, a feeling that, to quote the old hymn, this world is not our home. That inner voice ever troubles us with the realization that we are all, finally, pilgrims and sojourners, strangers in a strange land.

Not surprisingly, most of us stay put. Better to suppress that nagging voice than to risk the dangers of the road. And yet, even if we do not go off on adventures ourselves, we are continually drawn to characters, both historical and fictional, who do. Although the taking of pilgrimages to holy shrines and sacred places has played a major role in most world religions (especially medieval Catholicism), today, only Islam maintains a strong and visible commitment to this ancient discipline. True, many modern Americans will take secular, consumer-driven pilgrimages to such places as Disney World or Graceland or Manhattan, while others will take more intellectual and aesthetic pilgrimages to Rome or to Athens or to Stratford-upon-Avon. A number of Jews and Christians will even make their way to the Holy Land. Still, something, I fear, has been lost. Perhaps it is that sense of messianic anticipation that converts the journey into a longing for higher purpose. Perhaps it is that willingness to be profoundly changed that transforms it into a voyage of self-discovery. Perhaps we simply insulate ourselves too much.

Resisting the Road

The Lord of the Rings, like all the great romances of the Middle Ages, is essentially a quest narrative. Here, however, we do not encounter a willing hero (like Homer's Odysseus) whose journey promises him both reward and rest; rather, we have an unwilling hero (like Virgil's Aeneas) who does not wish, at least initially, to leave his home and who, if he reaches the end of his quest, will not necessarily receive either rest or reward. Tolkien's hero, a Hobbit named Frodo Baggins who lives a peaceful life in the rustic, protected Shire, is the nephew of another Hobbit named Bilbo who had himself gone on an adventure nearly eighty years earlier. As Tolkien tells the tale in *The Hobbit*, Bilbo is recruited by

Gandalf the wizard and a group of enterprising Dwarfs to help them recover stolen treasure from a fierce dragon named Smaug. The bourgeois Bilbo, who desires only a simple, complication-free life, is anything but enthusiastic. Rather than take joy in the twists and turns of the Road, he spends the first half of his journey casting continual backward glances to his safe, warm, comfortable Hobbit hole. Though Bilbo will prove the hero of the expedition, and though he will return to his home (Bag End) a more courageous and cosmopolitan person, his "there and back again" adventure is, in the final analysis, more a Viking raid than a quest or pilgrimage. Whereas Frodo is profoundly tested and changed by his travels along the Road, Bilbo, like Phileas Fogg or Lewis Carroll's Alice, returns to his very "English" Shire and picks up exactly where he left off.

Actually, it is a bit more complicated than that. *The Lord of the Rings* begins with Bilbo's celebration of his 111th birthday and his decision to leave the Shire and go to Rivendell to spend his closing years with the Elves. It has taken him over seventy years, but Bilbo has finally realized that his adventure *did* change him and that he cannot remain forever in the Shire. The Road calls out to him one last time, and he must go. Deep down, he would like to bring his thirty-three-year-old nephew with him, but he knows that Frodo is not ready to leave his home and take to the Road. He tries to explain this to Gandalf, who was his guide on his adventure and who will soon become Frodo's guide on his:

> I want to see the wild country again before I die, and the Mountains; but [Frodo] is still in love with the Shire, with woods and fields and little rivers. He ought to be comfortable here [in Bag End]. (I.i.32)

And comfortable he remains, until he reaches his fiftieth year: the same age Bilbo had been when he had set off on his adventure. By then, a wrestling has begun within Frodo: part of him (his Bilbo side) is drawn to the Shire, to all that is safe and familiar; another part (what we might call his pilgrim side) yearns to leave, to experience the far-flung world. In the end, however, he is compelled to depart, for Bilbo has unwittingly left in his possession the Ring of Sauron, the Dark Lord. If Frodo does not take this Ring to Rivendell immediately, he risks destruction not only for himself but for the Shire and, ultimately, all of Middle-earth.

And so, whether he wishes it or not, Frodo is cast out onto the Road, forced to embark on a pilgrimage that he has long desired to take, but would never have had the courage or resolve to begin. But it will take him some time to really leave the Shire behind, to learn to think of himself as a true sojourner in a world that does not belong to him and that cannot, in any case, promise final rest. For the lesson that the journey is to teach us is not simply that it is good to go on pilgrimages, but that we are pilgrims. Travel does not simply "broaden our minds"; it offers us insight into our own status as resident aliens in a fallen world. The Bilbo we meet at the beginning of *The Lord of the Rings* has learned this lesson in part. It will be left to Frodo to learn it in full.

In his struggles to learn it, Frodo is helped by a chance meeting with a group of Elves who are heading for the Gray Havens, from which point they will leave Middle-earth and sail far to the West. They are, quite literally, exiles, for as Tolkien tells us in *The Silmarillion*, they are descended from Elves who forsook their true home in the West and set out East for Middle-earth. They were and are *meant* for the West, as we Sons of Adam and Daughters of Eve *were* meant for the Garden of Eden and now *are* meant for the New

Jerusalem. Like all the Elves in Middle-earth, these that Frodo meet harbor an inner sadness; about them there hangs a melancholy, elegiac mood. They want to stay, yet know they must leave. They love dearly that which they must lose ere long. Sooner or later, they and the memory of them will fade from Middle-earth.

From these serene but displaced beings, Frodo learns that he must not return to the Shire, for it can no longer afford him protection. Frodo muses sadly that he never expected such danger to reach "our own Shire"; whereupon he is sternly but kindly rebuked by the Elf Gildor:

> But it is not your own Shire. . . . Others dwelt here before hobbits were; and others will dwell here again when hobbits are no more. The wide world is all about you: you can fence yourselves in, but you cannot for ever fence it out. (I.iii.82)

Up until now, Frodo has attempted to insulate himself, like the "ugly American" who visits exotic countries without ever stepping out of his American cocoon. (These "ugly Americans" have, of course, always been with us; in the General Prologue to his *Canterbury Tales*, Chaucer describes a group of "bourgeois" craftsmen who have brought their own cook with them lest they be forced to adapt to foreign food!) Now Frodo must let go of all that is safe and familiar and fully embrace the Road. Now he must learn that sense of urgency that the apostle Paul learned (perhaps) from his long years of wandering: "What I mean, brothers, is that the time is short. From now on those who have wives should live as if they had none; those who mourn, as if they did not; those who are happy, as if they were not; those who buy something, as if it were not theirs to keep; those who use the things of the world, as if not engrossed in them. For this world in its present form is passing away" (1 Corinthians 7:29–31 NIV).

We do not learn such hard truths sitting at home in our easy chairs. We can only learn them on the Road.

SHASTA'S JOURNEY

Bilbo and Frodo have a hard time leaving a place where they have known much peace and contentment. Ironically, the hero of *The Horse and His Boy* has the opposite problem: he fears to leave a place where he has known neither peace nor contentment. Unique among the Chronicles, *The Horse and His Boy* focuses not on children from our world, but on two children who live in the heathen and tyrannical land of Calormen, which lies due south of Narnia. One of these children is an unhappy princess (Aravis) who decides to flee from a distasteful arranged marriage. The other is a poor Oliver Twist–like orphan (Shasta) who has been raised by a cruel and unloving fisherman. Though Shasta does not know for sure that the fisherman is not his real father, he has long suspected that he does not belong in this land, that his true destiny and real identity lie elsewhere. Something within him has always impelled him to strain his eyes northward, but he has as yet been unable to muster the courage or find the opportunity to escape.

Then, as it does to Frodo, a situation arises that all but forces Shasta to flee from his native village and set out on the Road. Shasta overhears disturbing news that, first, his "father" is not his real father, and second, that he is about to sell him into the service of an even harsher taskmaster. Liberated by this discovery that the home and father he has never been able to love are, in fact, neither, Shasta is placed in a position where going off on a pilgrimage seems not only the proper but the necessary thing to do. But he cannot endure the journey alone. As Frodo is assisted on his way by Gandalf, Sam, Aragorn, and many others, Shasta is helped by a talking Narnian horse (Bree) who was kidnapped while a foal and has lived the brutal life of a dumb warhorse in Calormen.

Bree helps strengthen Shasta's resolve to leave by not only promising to carry him on his back, but by filling his heart and mind with a vision of what lies at the end of the Road:

> The happy land of Narnia — Narnia of the heathery mountains and the thymy downs. Narnia of the many rivers, the plashing glens, the mossy caverns and the deep forests ringing with the hammers of the Dwarfs. Oh the sweet air of Narnia! An hour's life there is better than a thousand years in Calormen. (I.9).

Unconsciously paraphrasing Psalm 84:10, Bree depicts Narnia as a place that is vastly superior to Calormen. Life there is richer, fuller, closer to what life was meant to be. It is where all those who are truly free belong. Indeed, when Shasta confesses that he has always longed to go north, Bree responds: "'Of course you have. . . . That's because of the blood that is in you. I'm sure you're true northern stock'" (I.12).

If the truth be told, we are all, finally, of true northern stock. That's one of the things that fairy tales teach us: that we are all heroes or princesses in disguise. And if that is so, then we must all set out to discover who we truly are: not so we can become rich or successful in the debased modern, consumerist sense, but so that we can step into our true inheritance.

The Road is not a one-size-fits-all proposition, but it offers to those who embrace it the rare and precious gift of self-knowledge. It forces us to step outside that which is known — outside of our "comfort zone" we would say today — and, by so doing, strips us of all our masks and disguises and alter egos. It forces us to look unswervingly into the face of fear, of confusion, of loneliness, reduces us to our naked essence. And then, slowly, it makes us stronger and wiser.

In the end, Shasta will play an instrumental role in saving Narnia from invasion by Calormen, just as Frodo will play an instrumental role in saving Middle-earth from the iron tyranny of Sauron. But they cannot participate in that saving act until they become the kind of people who can play the role of willing (if flawed) hero. To help prepare them for this role, to help them achieve the necessary self-knowledge, they are each given a close, intimate traveling companion who so contrasts and complements them as to aid in their self-development. For Shasta that companion is Aravis, whose aristocratic upbringing and regal self-confidence help to wean him away from his narrow provincialism and his lack of any sense of social responsibility. For Frodo that companion is Sam, his rustic gardener, whose earthy common sense and cheerful practicality keep Frodo going when his idealism threatens to crumble under the weight of Sauron's evil. In this, Frodo and Sam bear a more than passing resemblance to literature's most famous master/servant, idealist/realist pair: Don Quixote and Sancho Panza.

On the Road, we cannot escape from ourselves, but we also cannot escape from our companions—at least without risking grave peril. The temptation to abandon the path to which we have been called is often a strong one, but we must nevertheless trust that the Lord of the Road knows what He is doing. All we can do is press on with faith, hope, and perseverance.

That is one of the rules of the Road.

CHAPTER TWO

RESPONDING
to the CALL

In the previous chapter, I spoke as if those who go off on pilgrimages do so of their own free will, but that is not the whole story. According to the book of Genesis, God begins His sacred narrative, His drama of redemption, by calling on an ordinary, nonheroic man to leave his home and take to the Road. The man's name is Abraham, or rather, it is Abram; it is God who changes his name, as He often does for those whom He calls out for a special purpose.

Indeed, God calls Abraham to abandon his home in favor of the Road on two separate occasions, first leaving Ur for Haran, and then leaving Haran for the land of Canaan. Abraham, like Bilbo and Frodo, is a reluctant pilgrim, but he goes nonetheless. He goes, the author of Hebrews tells us, because he has something that all travelers must have if they are to stay true to their pilgrimage—faith in the call and the one who calls:

> By faith Abraham, when called to go to a place he would later
> receive as his inheritance, obeyed and went, even though he did
> not know where he was going. By faith he made his home in
> the promised land like a stranger in a foreign country; he lived
> in tents, as did Isaac and Jacob, who were heirs with him of
> the same promise. For he was looking forward to the city with
> foundations, whose architect and builder is God. (11:8–10 NIV)

Abraham was perhaps the first believer to know with certainty
that this world is not our home, that we are only passing through
until we find that higher Road that leads to a higher city not built
by human hands. Yes, he longed for the Land of Promise with the
same passionate desire that drove Shasta north toward Narnia,
but he also seems to have known what Frodo and the Elves knew:
that there is no final resting place on this earth—and Middle-
earth, we must remember, *is* our earth, in the far distant days
before Men took over and God revealed himself to the Jews.

Not content only to call His creatures to brave the Road, the
Christian revelation tells us that God Himself came to earth and
dwelt—literally, "tabernacled," as in the Hebrews passage quoted
above—among us (John 1:14). Jesus took His ministry on the
Road, where, unlike the birds and the foxes, He had no place
to lay His head (Matthew 8:20). After Christ's ascension, two
new Abrahams were called, with instructions to—you guessed
it—take to the Road. They too had their names changed—from
Simon to Peter, from Saul to Paul—and they too understand that
we are "strangers and pilgrims" (1 Peter 2:11) and that "our citi-
zenship is in heaven" (Philippians 3:20 NKJV).

EMBRACING EUCATASTROPHE

Like Abraham, Peter, and Paul, Frodo is clearly chosen to carry the Ring, not only to Rivendell but to the Cracks of Doom in which it was forged. But he is not the only one who journeys under a calling. Sam, for all his practical, feet-on-the-ground wisdom, slowly comes to realize that he too has been called for the journey. At first, he volunteers partly to protect his master and partly because he has long desired to see the Elves; however, on the morning after he and Frodo meet with the Exiled Elves (see chapter 1), a new awareness of deeper designs and higher purposes awakens within the humble gardener. He tries to explain it to Frodo:

> I don't know how to say it, but after last night I feel different. I seem to see ahead, in a kind of way. I know we are going to take a very long road, into darkness; but I know I can't turn back. It isn't to see the Elves now, nor dragons, nor mountains, that I want — I don't rightly know what I want: but I have something to do before the end, and it lies ahead, not in the Shire. I must see it through, sir, if you understand me. (I.iv.85)

Passages like this one run throughout *The Lord of the Rings* like threads in a tapestry. Not only Sam and Frodo, but all nine members of the Fellowship — the eight "walkers" chosen by Elrond, Lord of the Elves at Rivendell, to accompany Frodo the Ring-bearer — grow in their awareness that their presence in the Fellowship is neither coincidental nor fully of their own choosing.

Nevertheless, it is, to me at least, Sam's growing awareness that is the most moving and the most profound. It is true that Frodo can be profitably compared to Israel in general and King David in particular. Frodo, like Israel and her most beloved king, seems to have been chosen not because he is rich or wise or powerful, but because he is the smallest of the small, a mere pawn in the midst of mighty leaders and nations (see 1 Corinthians 1:26–31). And yet, if this is true of Frodo, then it is even more true of Sam. Tolkien himself explained that he meant Sam to stand for all those privates and batmen (or orderlies) who humbly, faithfully, and doggedly served the needs of their World War I officers. He even referred to him at times as the chief hero of *The Lord of the Rings*. Sam stands as a promise that anyone — *anyone* — can be used of God for noble purposes. He stands further as a pledge that those called, no matter how simple, can gain a glimpse, no matter how fleeting, of the part they have been called to play in the divine drama. That is to say, they not only see clearly the Road they are on, but are granted an inkling of that longer Road that stretches backward to Abraham and forward to the Apocalypse.

For me, the central passage in Tolkien's long epic comes as Frodo and Sam are about to pass into Mordor, the dark and desolate land where Sauron and Mount Doom dwell. As they pause there on the threshold, Sam shares with Frodo a profound meditation on the nature of the Road and on the nature of stories. It is a speech to which we who live in an age that has lost both its sense of purpose and its sense of history — that knows neither where it came from nor where it is going — must carefully attend.

Sam and Frodo are living at the end of the Third Age. Behind them stretch ten millennia of mighty warriors, heroic battles, and timeless tales of adventure and self-sacrifice. But they are, of course, more than tales. They are the stage, the backdrop against which these two seemingly insignificant Hobbits act out their roles in the sacred narrative of Creation, Fall, and Redemption. Sam begins by reflecting back on those tales and those who lived through them:

The brave things in the old tales and songs, Mr. Frodo: adventures, as I used to call them. I used to think that they were things the wonderful folk of the stories went out and looked for, because they wanted them, because they were exciting and life was a bit dull, a kind of sport, as you might say. But that's not the way of it with the tales that really mattered, or the ones that stay in the mind. Folk seem to have been just landed in them, usually — their paths were laid that way, as you put it. But I expect they had lots of chances, like us, of turning back, only they didn't. And if they had, we shouldn't know, because they'd have been forgotten. We hear about those as just went on — and not all to a good end, mind you, at least not to what folk inside a story and not outside it call a good end. You know, coming home, and finding things all right, though not quite the same — like old Mr. Bilbo. But those aren't always the best tales to hear, though they may be the best tales to get landed in! I wonder what sort of a tale we've fallen into? (IV.viii.696)

As I hinted in the previous chapter, there is good reason to believe that Tolkien's vision of the Road and of the call matured during the seventeen years that separate *The Hobbit* from *The Lord of the Rings*: a period that includes those dark and desperate years during which England faced annihilation by the Nazis. Though Bilbo's journey had allowed Tolkien to recover for his age much of the old magic and many of the old virtues, it lacked the proper scope to encompass the full dimensions of choice and destiny that define Frodo's journey. To accomplish that would take a greater tale, one that could live up to Sam's high description.

In the greater tales, the ones that matter — the ones that change both us and our world — the heroes do not so much choose the Road, as the Road chooses them. For our part, we must be ready, prepared in season and out, to answer the call, whenever and however it comes. And we must be prepared to press on, trusting to an end that we often do not, perhaps cannot, see. It is easy to claim that we would have done what Abraham did, but that is only because we stand outside the story. We see the good end, the fulfillment that Abraham could not see from within the story.

Sam muses on these things, and then, in one of those flashes of pure clarification that come to all those who endure in a cause, he realizes that the tale he and Frodo have been landed in is not a thing isolated from the past, but marks the continuation and perhaps even culmination of a tale that began long ago in the First Age:

> "Why, to think of it, we're in the same tale still! It's going on. Don't the great tales never end?"
>
> "No, they never end as tales," said Frodo. "But the people in them come and go when their part's ended. Our part will end later—or sooner." (IV.viii.697)

I believe it was Pascal who said that only God can see the whole picture and every detail within the picture at the same time. In his moment of clarification, Sam sees that his individual call (and that of Frodo) is part of a larger tapestry in which each individual call works together to bring about the destined and hoped for end, what Tolkien liked to call the *eucatastrophe*: the good end that rises up, miraculously, out of what seemed, at first, to be defeat and death.

If we would be a part of that eucatastrophe, then we must be willing to trust the call, to enter the tale, to set our weary feet to the Road.

REEPICHEEP'S CALLING

The prologue to *The Lord of the Rings* informs us that Hobbits range between two and four feet in height. The tale itself teaches us that physical size is no determiner of moral courage. Not to be undone in this paradoxical yoking of tiny body and mighty spirit, Lewis presents us, in *The Voyage of the Dawn Treader*, with a heroic traveler who is far closer to two feet than to four. I speak, of course, of one of Lewis's two favorite Narnian characters (the other is Puddleglum): Reepicheep the mouse. Unlike Tolkien's three-foot Abrahams, whose callings take them to the Road, the call that comes to Lewis's two-foot Abraham takes him out to the high seas.

In brief, *The Voyage of the Dawn Treader* tells of how three earth children are pulled into Narnia and accompany King Caspian and his crew as they sail across the wide, uncharted Eastern Sea, in search of the seven lost lords of Narnia. The adventures are marvelous, and each of the children goes through trials that test and refine him. But what lends the novel both its heroic and spiritual aura is the special purpose that has impelled Reepicheep to join the crew.

While he was still in his cradle, Reepicheep tells us, a Dryad spoke over him the following cryptic rhyme:

> Where sky and water meet,
> Where the waves grow sweet,
> Doubt not, Reepicheep,
> To find all you seek,
> There is the utter East. (II.16)

Though Reepicheep still does not understand the full import of the Dryad's prophecy, he proclaims that the spell of it has been on him all his life. No matter the danger or the cost, Reepicheep is determined to seek out his destiny, to respond to a calling that he only partially understands. Whereas Reepicheep is depicted in the previous Chronicle (*Prince Caspian*) as a brave, courteous, somewhat headstrong knight (rather like Gawain in *Sir Gawain and the Green Knight*), here he suffers a sea change into something far richer and stranger: a more mystical, God-haunted knight who is willing (like Sir Galahad of the Grail legends) to pursue his divine vision wherever it takes him.

Like Frodo and Sam, Reepicheep's final goal is not to win glory and fame but to fulfill the destiny for which he was chosen: to seek out Aslan's Country (essentially, heaven), which lies, as the rhyme foretold, at the Utter East of the world.

> My own plans are made. While I can, I sail east in the *Dawn Treader*. When she fails me, I paddle east in my coracle. When she sinks, I shall swim east with my four paws. And when I can swim no longer, if I have not reached Aslan's country, or shot over the edge of the world in some vast cataract, I shall sink with my nose to the sunrise and Peepiceek will be head of the talking mice in Narnia. (XIV.184)

Like the true medieval knight that he is, Reepicheep vows that no suffering, no sacrifice will prevent him from being true to his high calling.

It is precisely this kind of earnest fortitude that impels Frodo, Sam, and the rest of the Fellowship forward and that keeps them on the path for which they were chosen. True, one of them, Boromir, slips off the path and betrays the others, but he redeems himself in the end, and his failure is more than made up for by the even greater earnestness and fortitude of a character who, like Reepicheep, shares the same strength of arm and purity of spirit as Sir Galahad: Boromir's brother, Faramir. Faramir, like Frodo and Sam, is an unlikely hero, for his father holds him in contempt and places all his hope in Boromir — but Faramir overcomes the stigma placed on him by his father and plays a key role in the overthrow of Sauron.

The relationship between Frodo's diminutive stature, Sam's folkish simplicity, and Faramir's despised status and their indomitable, seemingly inexhaustible courage is truly paradoxical. But then so is the relationship between our shortcomings and the destinies to which we are called. Through the choices and destinies of Frodo, Sam, and Faramir, we learn that those who fully and obediently respond to the call are neither slaves nor puppets. To the contrary, they are passionate pilgrims whose freedom and self-determination are increased and perfected by their willingness to be part of a tale that is bigger and grander than themselves.

To be part of a tale that really matters.

CHAPTER THREE

DANGERS *on the* ROAD

It didn't hit me until a second reading, but once it did, the effect was overwhelming. In *The Lord of the Rings*, the Road is more than a path: it is a character. In noting this, of course, I was merely learning a lesson that Frodo tells us Bilbo had tried to teach him:

> [Bilbo] used often to say there was only one Road; that it was like a great river: its springs were at every doorstep, and every path was its tributary. "It's a dangerous business, Frodo, going out your door," he used to say. "You step into the Road, and if you don't keep your feet, there is no knowing where you might be swept off to." (I.iii.72)

As Frodo and Sam—along with their two fellow Hobbits, Merry and Pippin—trudge their way to Rivendell, they quickly come to realize that the Road has a life of its own. It winds, bends, and turns in a thousand directions, ever ready to trap or mislead the unwary traveler. To set your feet to the Road is indeed a dangerous business, not only on account of the obstacles that you face along the way, but because the Road is akin to a living thing with which you must relate, struggle, and negotiate. It draws and lures you, tests and challenges you, either punishing or rewarding you for your troubles.

On the one hand, the journey of the four Hobbits and then of the nine walkers retraces the path that Bilbo and the Dwarfs take in *The Hobbit*: a journey from the Shire to Rivendell followed by a terrifying descent through the Misty Mountains and a trek through a strange forest. On the other hand, the journey of Frodo and company is far darker and more archetypal. Like *Pilgrim's Progress* or Wagner's Ring Cycle or the original Star Wars Trilogy, it makes powerful use of images, events, places, and character that embody universal joys and primal fears. We've all been on such journeys before—in our dreams . . . or our nightmares.

THREE TRIALS

Like Grail knights in an Arthurian romance, the Hobbits must pass through three tests, represented geographically by three distinct thresholds that they must cross before they can reach Rivendell. Each threshold not only marks the boundary between one place and the next, but the transition between innocence and experience as well. The first threshold they must cross is called (allegorically) the Hedge. Once past it, the Hobbits find themselves in the Old Forest—a name which is also strongly archetypal, especially when it is compared to the more place-specific names of the other two forests visited in *The Lord of the Rings*: Lothlórien and Fangorn. When Merry is asked if the stories about the Old

Forest are true, he responds that he does not believe all the tales about goblins and wolves, but then adds that

> The Forest *is* queer. Everything in it is very much more alive, more aware of what is going on, so to speak, than things are in the Shire. And the trees do not like strangers. They watch you. (I.vi.108)

There is something about the Old Forest that conjures up the dark, archetypal fears of childhood. It embodies all those unnamed and unnameable terrors that children are warned to avoid. "Don't stray too far from that which is safe and familiar," the warning goes. "Stay on *this* side of the Hedge and all will be well. Better to leave the unknown unknown than to risk coming face-to-face with the dark side."

But, of course, if we are to grow and mature, then we must face it: both the dark side without and the often darker side within. Up until now, the Shire has been a kind of walled garden, a refuge shielded from the outside world. Indeed, we learn later in the book that the Shire has *literally* been protected from the growing evil of Sauron by a group of Men known as the Rangers. Though the Shire-folk are unaware of it, the Rangers have made it possible for them to remain in a relative state of innocence, to enjoy their food, drink, and tobacco free from the knowledge of impending doom.

The four Hobbits who cross the Hedge into the Old Forest have yet to be really tempted, yet to experience or even understand the awe-ful choice between good and evil, darkness and light that is being made by the various inhabitants of Middle-earth. The Hedge marks in many ways a point of no return—not so much in the physical, geographical sense as in the emotional and spiritual sense. Once they pass it, they open themselves—of their own choice—to a kind of higher Beauty and Terror that they have never known. On the other side of the Hedge waits not only the intense Life and Joy of Tom Bombadil—a figure who combines the jolly old qualities of Father Christmas, Bacchus, and Falstaff—but the numinous dread and horror of the Barrow-wights, evil spirits who nearly chill Frodo's blood and who conjure in the reader a deeper, more primal fear than the trolls that Bilbo faces in *The Hobbit*. One of the secrets of the Road is that you can't have the Beauty without the Terror. It *is* a dangerous thing to walk out your door, but without risk there is no real development, no self-knowledge, no awareness of the choices that one must make.

The second threshold the Hobbits must pass is the town of Bree, which lies at the far eastern end of the Hobbit world: a point beyond which few Hobbits venture. While at Bree, the Hobbits stay at the Inn of the Prancing Pony, a locale that reminds one less of a British pub—like Lewis and Tolkien's beloved Eagle and Child—than it does a saloon from a Hollywood Western (itself revisited by George Lucas in the famous bar scene in *Star Wars*). For Bree is nothing less than a Border Town (it houses Men, Hobbits, and Dwarfs alike), a rough and tumble "meeting place for the idle, talkative, and inquisitive . . . and a resort of Rangers and other wanderers" (I.ix.147). In fact, it is here that the Hobbits meet the chief of the Rangers, Aragorn, and begin to have their eyes opened to what the world is like outside the Shire. Guided by Aragorn, the Hobbits make their way through dangerous terrain, until they cross a third threshold, the Ford of Bruinen.

On the western side of the Ford, the Hobbits nearly fall prey to the Black Riders, nine deadly Wraiths who were once kings of Men but who were corrupted by the power of the Ring and now seek it out for their relentless master, Sauron. The Black

Riders are one of the most powerful embodiments in all literature of "that which is most to be feared," an undead state of perpetual misery devoid of all life, hope, and joy. On the eastern side, they are welcomed into Rivendell, a hidden valley that has the timeless and ethereal qualities of Shangri La. In complete contrast to the Black Riders, Rivendell embodies that which all mortals desire, a Garden of Eden setting where there is neither time nor age nor decay. What we only glimpse in the contrast between Tom Bombadil and the Barrow-wights, we see brought to fullness in the deeper contrast between Rivendell and the Black Riders. The Road leads us through both, forcing us to see the contrast and to choose wisely on which side we will fall.

It is a contrast that will be played out again as the full company of nine (the Fellowship of the Ring) crosses the most deadly threshold of all: the locked and hidden gate that opens to the Orc-infested Mines of Moria. Here, beneath the Misty Mountains, deep in the bowels of the earth, they must meet and overcome the overwhelming power and evil of the Balrog, a fire demon that had been awakened from sleep by the greed of Dwarfs who dug too deep. Gandalf defeats the Balrog, but in the struggle is himself cast into the abyss and falls into darkness. With his loss, Aragorn and Frodo are forced to take on more responsibility and to make decisions they had never thought they would have to make. The experienced Ranger and the inexperienced Hobbit, both of whom had been content to be led by Gandalf, emerge from Moria in a state of utter despair and confusion. But the tragic episode starts in them a process that results in a greater capacity for leadership and self-sacrifice than they had previously known.

Since the *Odyssey*, nearly every epic hero has had to face at some point in his journey-quest the archetypal Descent into the

Underworld. In the case of Virgil's *Aeneid*, Aeneas enters the realm of Hades as a grieving and defeated Trojan, but emerges as the Father of the Roman Empire. In the case of Dante's *Inferno*, Dante enters the yawning pit of Hell as a confused and despairing pilgrim who has lost his way, but emerges as a renewed believer who has regained his purpose, vision, and calling. Tolkien cleverly combines these epic trajectories in the characters of Frodo and Aragorn—and, to a lesser extent, the other members of the Fellowship. The crossing of the threshold of Moria and of Gandalf's death galvanizes the Ring-bearer and the Ranger and equips them to fulfill their high destiny: for Frodo, to face the nihilistic despair of Mordor and complete his task; for Aragorn, to become the anticipated High King of Middle-earth who will restore peace and justice to the land.

The transformation is a slow and painful one, but the Road is merciful. Soon after the Fellowship escapes from Moria, the Road leads them into an enchanted forest that is as timeless and ethereal as Rivendell. Here, in the sacred wood of Lothlórien, they meet the Lady Galadriel, a Queen of Light who stands in contrast to the baleful influence of the Dark Lord Sauron. Like the Delectable Mountains in *Pilgrim's Progress*, Lórien is a place of refreshment, a way station for the weary pilgrim. It is another secret of the Road that no matter how dark and difficult the path, there are always inns along the way where the sojourner may rest his head ... even if it is only for a night.

FOLLOWING THE SIGNS

Like the members of Tolkien's Fellowship, Eustace and Jill, the two earth children who are drawn into Narnia in the opening chapter of *The Silver Chair*, must also cross the threshold from innocence to experience, facing along the way the dangers of the Road and even suffering their own Descent into the Underworld. The two children are commissioned by Aslan to rescue Prince Rilian, Son of King Caspian, who was kidnapped by the Emerald Witch and is being held prisoner in her underground lair. As the divine commissioning of Lewis's two "walkers" is more explicit than that of Tolkien's nine, Lewis is able to factor into his quest narrative something that can only remain implicit in *The Lord of the Rings*. Whereas Frodo and Aragorn only have a vague notion of how they are to proceed in their mission, Jill—and, through her, Eustace—is given very strict and clear orders on how she is to conduct her quest for the lost prince.

Before sending her into Narnia to begin her journey, Aslan has Jill memorize four Signs (or clues) that will help her and Eustace to find Rilian. Once he is satisfied with her recitation of the Signs, Aslan leaves Jill with the following warning:

> Remember, remember, remember the Signs. Say them to yourself when you wake in the morning and when you lie down at night, and when you wake in the middle of the night. And whatever strange things may happen to you, let nothing turn your mind from following the Signs. And secondly, I give you a warning. Here on the mountain I have spoken to you clearly. I will not often do so down in Narnia. Here on the mountain, the air is clear and your mind is clear; as you drop down into Narnia, the air will thicken. Take great care that it does not confuse your mind. And the Signs which you have learned here will not look at all as you expect them to look, when you meet them there. That is why it is so important to know them by heart and pay no attention to appearances. Remember the Signs and believe the Signs. Nothing else matters. (II.21)

Lewis certainly means the Signs to represent, in part, the Old and New Testaments: in particular, the Law of Moses (on which Joshua is equally exhorted to meditate day and night) and the teachings of Jesus (which many a child in Sunday school or Catechism class will be expected to memorize). In the Judeo-Christian revelation, such scriptural verses are meant to act as guideposts along the Road, markers to keep us on track lest we fall by the wayside—as, we saw above, Dante does at the outset of the *Divine Comedy*. "Thy word," proclaims the psalmist, "is a lamp unto my feet, and a light unto my path" (119:105).

Lewis, however, adds a subtle twist to the words of the psalmist. Although the Call is clear and forceful when it first comes to us in its original purity, as we journey farther along the Road—away from the initial Light of the Call—things grow fainter and less clear: for, in our present state, we see not clearly but "through a glass, darkly" (1 Corinthians 13:12). This is another danger of the Road, that, when the clarity of the mountaintop vision gives way to the mist of the valley or the darkness of the cave, we will lose our focus and wander aimlessly. Remember that both Moses' law and Jesus' longest sermon were delivered from mountains. "'Follow your star,'" Dante is advised as he labors through Hell, 'for if in all / of the sweet life I saw one truth shine clearly, / you cannot miss your glorious arrival'" (XV.55–7).

At several points in *The Silver Chair*, Eustace and Jill lose sight of that Star, and the Signs become muddled in their minds. When they do, the Road sweeps them off on dangerous detours, and they are forced to see and experience things that they would rather have avoided. Fooled by the Emerald Witch—who fills their minds with vague, inordinate desires that blot out the Signs—they confuse an inn of refreshment with a den of vipers and are nearly eaten by cannibalistic giants. This error forces them in turn to make a Descent into the Underground Kingdom of the Witch that is far longer, darker, and drearier than the path Aslan had intended them to take. Finally, fooled a second time by the Witch, they come close to doubting the very existence of Narnia, the sun, and Aslan himself.

When I finish *The Silver Chair*, and turn my attention back to *The Lord of the Rings*, I am reminded of a more spiritual danger that is found in Tolkien but is less obvious than the physical danger posed by the Balrog or the Orcs. As odd as it may seem, one of the greatest obstacles that the members of the Fellowship, or any pilgrim for that matter, must face is the temptation to cease believing in the Road—to embrace a postmodern, existential nihilism that says that there is neither beginning nor end, that we are all adrift in a world without Purpose, Direction, or Call. In short, that there really is no Road, or, if there is, that it leads nowhere.

When the Fellowship is broken apart at the end of Book II, both Frodo and Aragorn are afflicted by doubt and by a paralyzing fear that they have utterly lost their way. What restores to them their faith and position of leadership is a renewed sense that they must trust to the Road laid out before them and to the Call that is uniquely theirs. Strengthened by this new resolve, they press on, each to his appointed end.

May we who live in a modern-postmodern society where the air is thick and the Road often unclear share in their courage and resolve.

the END *of the* ROAD

Pope John Paul II spoke prophetic words when he accused the modern world of embracing a "culture of death." But that, I think, is not the whole story. Though the troubling issues of abortion, euthanasia, and the death penalty are ones the Western world has yet to deal with fully, there is another aspect of the "culture of death" that, to my mind at least, has proven a stumbling block to both liberal Democrats and conservative Republicans, secular humanists and evangelical Christians. I speak of the fact that our society is strongly, if not pathologically, death aversive. When our grandparents lie in a hospital room close to death, we refuse to discuss their coming demise or give them the opportunity to speak their final, parting words. We fool ourselves into believing that we will live forever, and convert diet, exercise, and health itself into something that borders dangerously on idolatry.

Doctors take as their enemy not disease, pain, and suffering, but death itself—a losing battle, if there ever was one! Although the hospice program has helped tremendously in teaching our society to accept death and to be unafraid to look it in the face, it can hardly reverse, on its own, an aversion that everything in our society seems intent on nurturing.

Tolkien held, as did Lewis, the orthodox Christian belief that suicide is a grave sin, one that is generally motivated by an over-indulgence in pride and despair. Indeed, when Denethor, the Steward of Gondor, allows just such an indulgence to push him to the brink of self-immolation, Gandalf attempts, unsuccessfully, to dissuade him from the act with these words:

> Authority is not given to you, Steward of Gondor, to order the hour of your death . . . and only the heathen kings, under the domination of the Dark Power, did thus, slaying themselves in pride and despair, murdering their own kin to ease their own death. (V.vii.835)

Lewis, who, like Tolkien, served in World War I, understood well the divine command to remain at the post to which God has called us. In *The Horse and His Boy*, Aravis, raised by the kind of heathen kings to whom Gandalf refers, comes herself close to the brink of suicide, but is turned aside from this path by a talking Narnian horse named Hwin. Saved by Hwin's intervention, Aravis realizes in time that "the fear of death has disordered [her] reason and subjected [her] to delusions" (III.35). It is clear from the narrative that leads up to her attempted suicide that Aravis, like Denethor, is motivated by pride and despair—but the fact that Aravis highlights her fear of death as being the main contributing factor to her near-fatal decision is instructive.

When we fear something, we tend to misunderstand it, and, if we do not clear up that misunderstanding, fear generally gives way to hate and to the creation of an adversarial relationship. This may help explain why the fear of death that lies at the core of our modern civilization manifests itself *both* in demands for the "right to die" and in even stronger, seemingly contradictory demands that every form of medical treatment (no matter how extreme) must be expended on every patient (no matter how old or infirm).

In the midst of this confusion, Tolkien and Lewis can offer some advice that can help us, I believe, to accept the inevitability and even goodness of death without pushing us to the brink of euthanasia on demand: advice that can help our society say, with St. Paul, that though we desire to depart and be with the Lord, we shall, for the sake of God and of others, remain in the flesh (Philippians 1:23–4).

THE GIFT OF DEATH

Briefly in Appendix A of *The Lord of the Rings*, and at much greater length in *The Silmarillion*, Tolkien suggests, quite stunningly, that from the beginning Ilúvatar (the Creator) not only intended for Men to be mortal but granted this mortality as a boon (Tolkien calls it the "Gift of Men"). Unlike the Elves, who are immortal but whose lives are inextricably bound to the earth, Men are destined someday to leave behind the world and move on to a higher destiny. What exactly this destiny will be is unknown, not only to Men and Elves, but to the Valar (or angelic beings) who watch over the world and help to regulate it. Ilúvatar alone knows what their final end will be; as for those who must suffer mortality and take that final journey, they are left only with hope in the promises of Ilúvatar.

In tandem with his "gift" of mortality, Ilúvatar had granted them as well a spirit of restlessness that they might never feel quite comfortable or at home in this world. For Tolkien, that is to say, our status as pilgrims and sojourners is natural to us; it has been "hardwired" in our genes by the Creator. Why, then, do we fear death if it is truly a gift from the One who made us? Because, Tolkien explains, Sauron—and *his* Dark Master, Morgoth—has so corrupted the gift and our understanding of it that death has become shrouded in darkness, mystery, and dread, a thing to be feared and avoided rather than embraced at the proper time.

On their way to Mordor, Frodo and Sam meet up with Faramir, the wise and gentle son of Denethor, who, like Aragorn, is one of the few remaining descendants of a group of men known as the Númenoreans. During the Second Age of Middle-earth, the Númenoreans had been rewarded by Ilúvatar and the Valar with long, though not immortal lives and had been granted an Edenic island (Númenor) to dwell on in peace and prosperity. Unfortunately, the Númenoreans, corrupted by Sauron, came to envy the immortality of the Elves and the Valar and sought to win it for themselves. As a punishment, they and their island were destroyed, and only a remnant survived to reestablish their kingdom on the less-Edenic soil of Middle-earth. There, a group of them built the Kingdom of Gondor, but soon they fell into the same sins as their ancestors.

In words that call up images of ancient Egypt but that bespeak as well our own age, Faramir explains to Frodo and Sam what happened to the kings of Gondor:

> Death was ever present, because the Númenoreans still, as they had in their old kingdom [of Númenor], and so lost it, hungered after endless life unchanging. Kings made tombs more splendid

than houses of the living, and counted old names in the rolls of
their descent dearer than the names of sons. Childless lords sat
in aged halls musing on heraldry; in secret chambers withered
men compounded strong elixirs, or in high cold towers asked
questions of the stars. (IV.v.663–4)

In their contradictory lusting after personal immortality and
abandonment of procreation, the fallen Kings of Gondor come
disturbingly close to our own modern Western world, with its lust
for medical breakthroughs, no matter the ethical cost, coupled
with a sharply declining birthrate.

In contrast to these death-aversive kings, Tolkien depicts for
us the noble and peaceful death of Aragorn, who accepts his demise and embraces it. His wife, Arwen—the elven daughter of
Elrond who gives up her immortality to marry Aragorn—begs
him to live yet longer, but he comforts her, saying:

Take counsel with yourself, beloved, and ask whether you
would indeed have me wait until I wither and fall from my high
seat unmanned and witless. Nay, lady, I am the last of the Númenoreans and the latest King of the Eldar Days; and to me has
been given not only a span thrice that of Men of Middle-earth,
but also the grace to go at my will, and give back the gift. Now,
therefore, I will sleep. (Appendix A.v.1037)

And when Arwen exclaims in her grief that Ilúvatar's gift is a bitter one to receive, Aragorn comforts her further with words to
which we moderns would do well to attend:

So it seems. . . . But let us not be overthrown at the final test,
who of old renounced the Shadow and the Ring. In sorrow
we must go, but not in despair. Behold! We are not bound for

ever to the circles of the world, and beyond them is more than memory. Farewell! (Appendix A.v.1038)

Aragorn's death is neither a form of "passive euthanasia," nor does it mask a death wish. Rather, it signifies Aragorn's acceptance of his own mortality and his refusal to claw desperately for every last breath of life, as though death were an unmitigated evil. Of course, few of us are granted Aragorn's boon "to go at [his] will" — a boon granted to Christ, who gave up His spirit on the cross, rather than having it taken from Him by slow asphyxiation or the breaking of His legs. Nevertheless, Aragorn's death can serve as an object lesson for an age that is almost obsessive-compulsive in its desire to perpetually hold death at arm's length.

At this point, attentive readers may be shaking their heads in disbelief that Tolkien would suggest that mortality was a gift granted by the Creator from the beginning, rather than a direct result of the fall of man — a doctrine that Tolkien, as an orthodox Catholic, firmly believed in. As a matter of fact, Tolkien seemed himself to have been disturbed by this, and even suggested at one point that the seeming discrepancy between Genesis 3 and *The Silmarillion* might be explained by the fact that *The Silmarillion* was written from an elvish, rather than a human or divinely revealed point of view (see #212 in *The Letters of J. R. R. Tolkien*, edited by Humphrey Carpenter). Still, the force of Tolkien's myth of the origin of Man's mortality reverberates through his grand narrative, and causes the reader (at least *this* reader) to wonder if the death ushered in by our eating of the Fruit of the Knowledge of Good and of Evil was not spiritual rather than physical.

Regardless of how we read *The Silmarillion* and Genesis 3, we can still learn from Tolkien a vital spiritual truth: death is the doorway through which we escape the limits of our physical world and enter into the eternity of heaven—something that Tolkien's Elves will never be able to do. Whatever the situation was in our pre-fallen state, on this side of Eden, we must first die if we are to be reborn, resurrected, and made new: a truth that Tolkien highlights in *The Lord of the Rings* by staging no less than three dramas of death and resurrection—Gandalf is reborn after his fight with the Balrog; Frodo is "killed" by Shelob the spider but then returns from his sleep of death; Aragorn treads the Paths of the Dead and returns alive and victorious.

ASLAN'S COUNTRY

The Chronicles of Narnia, though smaller in scope than Tolkien's vast epic, also touches on the grand theme of the nature and purpose of man's mortality. In *The Last Battle*, the darkest and most esoteric of the seven novels, Lewis recounts the tribulation, destruction, and final judgment of Narnia and its inhabitants. It seems almost cruel that Lewis would force his readers to witness the death of the land that they have so come to love, but he has a message to deliver, and it is one that he wants his readers—especially his young readers—to understand and accept. And that message is simply this:

All worlds draw to an end; except Aslan's own country. (VIII.89)

Though Jill, who is brought to Narnia along with Eustace to help stem the tide of destruction, knows that our world will end, she harbors a secret hope that Narnia will never end—that it will go on forever and ever. The line quoted above is the answer Jill receives when she shares her hope, an answer that is soon confirmed by a series of events that lead to the (literal) unmaking of Narnia by apocalyptic forces unleashed by Aslan.

But it is not only the death of Narnia that we are forced to endure in *The Last Battle*. In the closing chapters of the novel, we learn that all but one of the earth children whom we have come to know and love in the preceding six novels have died in a train wreck and have been transported to the dying Narnia in the final seconds of life. After first watching in awe and wonder as Aslan judges the talking beasts and Narnia falls into darkness, and then witnessing with greater awe and wonder the glories of Aslan's Country, the children—only two of whom have grown old since their adventures in Narnia—fully expect that Aslan will send them back to the earth as he had done so many times before. In the past, they had been eager, if somewhat sad, to return to England, but now all they wish to do is remain forever in Aslan's Country. It is therefore with great joy that they receive Aslan's startling news:

> There *was* a real railway accident. . . . Your father and mother and all of you are—as you used to call it in the Shadow-Lands— dead. The term is over: the holidays have begun. The dream is ended: this is the morning. (XVI.183)

If we take this lovely and haunting passage and combine it with Lewis's breathtaking descriptions of the beauty and freedom of Aslan's Country, I believe we will come very close to understanding Tolkien's admittedly strange suggestion that death is Ilúvatar's Gift to Men. For it is precisely *because* death releases us from bondage to this world and opens forth to us a higher and nobler destiny, that Tolkien can assert that death is a good thing. As St. Paul himself expresses it: "For now we see through a glass, darkly; but then face to face" (1 Corinthians 13:12). We have been convinced by the Enemy that death is the Shadow, when it is, in fact, *our* world that is the Shadow. It is not death but life that is the dream; on the other side waits not night but morning.

In the opening chapter of *The Lord of the Rings*, Tolkien introduces the theme of the Road with these lilting words that promise adventure and romance:

> The Road goes ever on and on
>> Down from the door where it began.
> Now far ahead the Road has gone,
>> And I must follow, if I can. (I.i.35)

In the closing chapter, he returns to this poem, but infuses it with a new kind of adventure and a new kind of yearning for a Road beyond the Road that will lead us to a new world:

> Still round the corner there may wait
>> A new road or a secret gate;
> And though I oft have passed them by,
>> A day will come at last when I
> Shall take the hidden paths that run
>> West of the Moon, East of the Sun. (VI.ix.1005)

PART TWO

The Classical Virtues

the COURAGE
to ENDURE

When Dante sat down to write his great medieval Catholic epic, he had to decide, first, who he would choose as his guide through hell and purgatory. Though most Christian writers faced with such a dilemma would have chosen a Christian saint — perhaps one of the apostles or Augustine or Francis or Aquinas — Dante deliberately chose a pagan poet (Virgil) for his guide. By so doing, Dante asserted his belief — shared by most of the great Catholic writers, up to and including J. R. R. Tolkien and his Anglo-Catholic friend, C. S. Lewis — that the ancient Greeks and Romans, though unable to attain salvation on the basis of their merit alone, were capable of understanding and seeking after virtue. That is to say, though they were fallen and in need of grace, they were not utterly depraved. And for Dante, as for Tolkien and Lewis, it was quite clear what those pre-Christian virtues were. They consisted, at their highest, in four distinct virtues that were referred to collectively as the classical or cardinal virtues: Justice, Temperance (or Self-control), Wisdom (or Prudence), and Courage (or Fortitude). Readers of the *Republic* will immediately recognize these four virtues as the ones, so Plato argues, that constitute the enlightened soul and that must operate in society if the just state is to survive and thrive. These four virtues—that were known and practiced, if imperfectly, by peoples who lacked the Scriptures but had access to God's general revelation—were distinguished by Dante and the church from the three theological virtues (Faith, Hope, and Love) which were not known, at least in their fullness, until the Christian revelation. Or, as Lewis explains it succinctly in book III, chapter 2 of *Mere Christianity*, "The 'Cardinal' [virtues] are those which all civilized people recognize; the 'Theological' are those which, as a rule, only Christians know about."

In the first section of this book, I concentrated on the Road and our status as pilgrims on that Road. In the two sections that follow, I will shift my focus to the virtues such pilgrims must possess if they are to endure the dangers along the way and carry out their calling to its proper end. As such, the two sections that follow will be slightly more pragmatic than the first, narrowing the scope to real-life actions and motivations. In the former, we will study closely each of the four classical virtues; in the latter, we will take up the three theological virtues, along with a fourth (friendship) that Tolkien and Lewis raised to a level midway between the classical and the theological. Throughout, we will pay careful attention to how Tolkien and Lewis so revived and reincarnated these eight virtues in their work as to make them relevant again for an age that has in many ways sunk beneath the pagans in its understanding of virtue. As already stated in the introduction, our public schools seem equipped only to teach three "virtues": tolerance, multiculturalism, and environmentalism. With the help of Tolkien and Lewis, I hope to posit a vision of virtue that is more dynamic, lasting, and flexible. (Ralph C. Wood also uses the virtues to structure part of his argument in his excellent study, *The Gospel According to Tolkien*. See Appendix A.)

PRESSING ON TO MORDOR

In book III, chapter 2 of *Mere Christianity*, Lewis states that without courage (fortitude) we will not be able to practice for long any of the other virtues. For that reason, and because courage is probably the first virtue that most people associate with *The Lord of the Rings* and, to a lesser extent, The Chronicles of Narnia, I will begin there. According to the American Heritage Dictionary, fortitude is a "strength of mind that allows one to endure pain or adversity with courage." Though I rarely quote the dictionary in my writing, and even gently chide my students when they do so in their own, I find this definition to be so apt—not only to the full classical understanding of fortitude but to the way that virtue manifests itself in *The Lord of the Rings* and the Chronicles—that I've decided to waive my usual "no dictionary rule."

To first-time readers of Tolkien's epic, perhaps the strongest impression that it leaves is one of length: slow, painstaking length. Tolkien, who loved to take long, rambling country walks with Lewis, had already factored a great deal of walking into *The Hobbit*, but in that lighter, more fairy-tale-like prequel, the daily hikes of Bilbo and company seem less arduous and taxing than those in *The Lord of the Rings*. Frodo's slow-motion trek to Rivendell, the Fellowship's exhausting passage from Rivendell to Lothlórien,

Aragorn's lengthy chase of the Orcs who have kidnapped Merry and Pippin, Frodo's grueling journey into the heart of Mordor: all seem to reflect less Tolkien's joyous memories of walking tours than his darker memories of the incessant marches he was forced to endure as a foot soldier in World War I.

Tolkien has, of course, been criticized for "boring" his readers with extended and excruciating descriptions of each and every march. (In his typically affable-irascible style, Tolkien once responded that the real problem with *The Lord of the Rings* was that it was too *short*!) Nevertheless, despite the understandable impatience of modern readers, the fact remains that the long length and slow pace of *The Lord of the Rings* are central to Tolkien's overall vision. For the true courage of the nine walkers (especially Frodo) consists *precisely* in their endurance, their ability to press on no matter the pain or adversity. They are all given numerous chances to turn back and abandon the quest. Instead, they slog on day after weary day, facing every obstacle with quiet determination.

Such courage through endurance has become a foreign thing to our modern civilization, which demands to have everything *now*, without having to wait or suffer for it. Yes, college students will press on for four or more years to get their degree, but they expect to live well while they do it, and they rarely deny themselves any pleasures along the way. When they graduate and get married, they expect to have immediately everything that their parents have *now*—as opposed to what their parents had when they first got married. Even as they age, they rarely deny themselves the most up-to-date technological equipment; rather than save enough money to buy a new car, they buy the new car *now* and pay for it later. This impulsive, consumer-driven behavior may seem at first to have nothing to do with the issue at hand, but it is, in fact, closely related. Only those who possess fortitude can bear to have their desires mortified for a higher cause; only the truly courageous can endure the loss (permanent *or* temporary) of those things that they consider their right and their due.

As he approaches Mount Doom, Frodo finds that the Ring has robbed him not only of his joy and peace but of his most basic sensual pleasures:

> No taste of food, no feel of water, no sound of wind, no memory of tree or grass or flower, no image of moon or star are left to me. I am naked in the dark, Sam, and there is no veil between me and the wheel of fire [the Eye of Sauron]. I begin to see it even with my waking eyes, and all else fades. (VI.iii.916)

The stripping that Frodo must endure if he is to complete his mission is almost unbearable; yet still, he presses on. He never says, "I have done and suffered enough and now want someone else to take over." He most certainly never complains that it is "unfair" that he should have to bear the brunt of the work. His mind is fixed on a single goal: getting the Ring to Mount Doom. What is "best for him" or what will "help him to grow in his career" are irrelevant. All that matters is that he fulfill his duty.

Significantly, at exactly the same time Frodo is courageously crawling toward Mount Doom, Aragorn reaches the Black Gate of Mordor, where he hopes to lead an attack on Sauron's forces that will distract the Eye of the Enemy from Frodo and Sam. In taking on this task, Aragorn also places duty above momentary pleasure, the needs of the many over his own personal needs and desires. He knows that he is leading his men on a suicidal assault, but instead of pausing to ponder what course of action will earn him a promotion or best aid in his "self-actualization," he rouses the spirits of his men with bold and fearless words:

> We must walk open-eyed into the trap, with courage, but small
> hope for ourselves. For, my lords, it may well prove that we
> ourselves shall perish utterly in a black battle far from the living
> lands; so that even if [the Dark Tower] be thrown down, we
> shall not live to see a new age. But this, I deem, is our duty. And
> better so than to perish nonetheless—as we surely shall, if we sit
> here—and know as we die that no new age shall be. (V.ix.862)

Many today will endure suffering if it will ensure them a rich
reward or gain them fame. Aragorn is willing to die—forgotten
and unwept—in a black valley far from the living lands. He is
willing not only to sacrifice himself, but to do so without thanks
or recognition.

At the very end of the epic, Frodo too comes to this realization,
that those who suffer and sacrifice often reap no direct reward, at
least in this life, for their labors:

> I tried to save the Shire, and it has been saved, but not for me. It
> must often be so, Sam, when things are in danger: some one has
> to give them up, lose them, so that others may keep them. (VI.
> ix.1006)

Here Frodo comes closest to the courage shown by Christ Himself, when He laid down His life for those who mocked and rejected Him. True courage is not so much about self-glorification
as it is about self-emptying: being willing to be the bridge over
which others may cross to safety. It does not rest on anything so
flimsy or ephemeral as "self-esteem," but proceeds instead out
of an inner integrity that knows who it is—and where it is going—and can therefore fix its gaze outward rather than inward.

Like Christ, Frodo and Aragorn have a firm sense of the higher mission that has been bequeathed them, and it empowers them with the strength to endure. Theirs is a fortitude we could use far more of today.

ASLAN'S COURAGE

Not surprisingly, the Chronicles come even closer than *The Lord of the Rings* to depicting Christ-like courage, for, unlike Tolkien's epic romance, Lewis's seven fairy tales include a character who is not only Christ-like, but who *is* Christ Himself—at least, Lewis explained, as He might have appeared had He become incarnate in a magical world of talking animals and living trees. In *The Lion, the Witch and the Wardrobe*, Aslan, the Lion-King of Narnia and the Son of the Emperor-Beyond-the-Sea, willingly sacrifices himself to buy back the life of a treacherous child named Edmund. He does so, not from a position of weakness, but from one of strength and integrity. When he surrenders himself to the White Witch, he knows that with a single swipe of his claw he could kill a dozen of her minions, but instead he endures patiently the pain and adversity laid out before him. With supernatural fortitude, he accepts without complaint both the physical pain of being murdered on the Stone Table and the perhaps greater emotional pain of being mocked, humiliated (his hair is shorn off), and bound with a muzzle. Throughout the full ordeal, Aslan neither speaks nor cries out: his courage lies deeper than words or threats or recriminations. As Lucy, the most spiritually sensitive of the children, looks on the face of the shorn lion, she realizes to her surprise that his face now looked "braver, and more beautiful, and more patient than ever" (XIV.151).

In chapter 8 of *Orthodoxy*, G. K. Chesterton sagely notes that "of all creeds, Christianity [alone] has added courage to the virtues of the Creator. For the only courage worth calling courage must necessarily mean that the soul passes a breaking point — and does not break." Christ, Chesterton adds, was willing to do what no god had ever done before: allow His back to be pressed against a wall. Just so, Aslan allows the full weight of the White Witch's wrath to fall upon him, and, in a manner analogous, Frodo and Aragorn bear upon themselves the crushing weight of the Ring of Power and the forces of Mordor. All three are driven beyond the breaking point, yet none of them breaks: though Frodo does in the end succumb to the Ring and must be saved by a higher providence (as indeed, must we all!). We who would live courageous lives in the midst of a fast-food, throwaway world would do well to look to Frodo, Aragorn, and Aslan, all of whom reflect the example of Christ, which St. Paul exhorted the early church to follow:

> Looking unto Jesus the author and finisher of our faith; who for the joy that was set before him endured the cross, despising the shame, and is set down at the right hand of the throne of God. For consider him that endured such contradiction of sinners against himself, lest ye be wearied and faint in your minds. (Hebrews 12:2–3)

Again, fortitude is more about endurance than anything else; it is about fixing our minds on the prize — not the earthly one, but the heavenly — and not allowing our hearts to grow faint.

There is another reason why it is helpful to think of courage in terms of endurance, one that is also central to Lewis and Tolkien's understanding of what it takes to be a hero in the world of faerie or in our own more mundane world. In the introductory chapter of *The Problem of Pain*, Lewis makes a vital distinction between two different types of fear that most of us will encounter at some time in our lives. The first type is fear proper, the fear we feel in the presence of a wild animal or an enemy soldier that threatens to kill us. The second, though referred to by the same word, is actually qualitatively different than the first. This experience, that Lewis (after Rudolph Otto) calls *numinous* fear, occurs when we come into the presence of something supernatural, something that does not so much threaten us physically as overwhelm our spirit—the type of fear we might feel if we stood in the midst of a graveyard at midnight, or, more to the point, the type of fear that Moses felt when he stood before the burning bush (Exodus 3) or Isaiah felt when he saw the Lord, high and mighty, sitting upon His throne (Isaiah 6).

In keeping with Lewis's distinction, Tolkien suggests in *The Lord of the Rings* that the single greatest act of courage performed by Aragorn is not displayed on the battlefield or in the Mines of Moria or before the Black Gates of Mordor. Above and beyond all his other noble deeds, Aragorn shows the greatest fortitude, the greatest endurance when he rides willingly the Paths of the Dead and calls upon the cursed spirits of those who had betrayed his great ancestor, Isildur, at the end of the Second Age. Though the spirits of the Oathbreakers cannot harm Aragorn in any physical sense, they threaten to unbalance his mind with dread and prostrate his spirit with terror. All that is within Aragorn dissuades him from treading this fearsome path; yet he takes it nonetheless, for it is his appointed path, and "no other road will serve" (V.ii.766).

CHAPTER SIX

TEMPERANCE
and TOBACCO

Most people, I believe, misunderstand Aristotle's notion of the "golden mean." They are aware that the ancient Greeks who helped lay the foundation of Western civilization believed that we should do all things in moderation ("nothing to excess"), but they tend to simplify this central Hellenic notion into that most banal of modern American cliches: I'll try anything once. That we must be tolerant and "open-minded" and willing to give anything a chance is most certainly *not* what Aristotle meant when he called on his fellow Greeks (in the *Nicomachean Ethics*) to seek the middle path. For Aristotle, virtuous behavior consists not in being "moderate" per se, but in finding "the mean between the extremes."

As Plato's "star pupil," Aristotle affirmed fully the four classical virtues of his master; however, he defined them in a slightly different way and from a slightly different perspective. In place of Plato's metaphysical definitions of the virtues, Aristotle offered a more practical way of understanding and practicing them. Aristotle viewed courage not as an imitation of the perfect Form or Idea of Courage that exists in the heavens, but as the middle state between the two extremes of cowardice and rashness. Thus, while cowardice betrays a *lack* of true courage, rashness (its polar opposite) betrays an *excess* of it. We all know that a coward does not possess courage, but we sometimes forget that the rash, headstrong man who charges into danger without control or forethought is equally bereft of the virtue of courage. To put it in terms of our last chapter, neither the one who lacks heart nor the one who lacks patience will long endure in the face of pain and adversity.

Courage does not mean adopting a "devil may care" attitude or rushing blindly into danger. Technically speaking, Boromir (the Prince of Gondor who attempts to steal the Ring from Frodo and is soon after killed by Orc arrows) does not possess the full classical virtue of fortitude. He is brave and strong and nearly impervious to pain, but he lacks the patient endurance that locates courage between the two extremes of cowardice and rashness. The same can be said of his father, Denethor, whose rash suicide reveals a strain of cowardice. In contrast to both, Boromir's brother (Faramir) displays a courage that is wise, just, and temperate; he never loses his focus, never falters, never allows excessive fear or passion to turn him from the path. It is precisely this kind of courage that first Bilbo and then Frodo learn as they endure the challenges and the dread fears that meet them along the Road.

In *The Last Battle*, Lewis pulls off something of a coup by embodying both Boromir and Faramir in a single character: Tirian, the last king of Narnia. When Tirian learns that evil is afoot in Narnia, he and his sidekick, Jewel the Unicorn, reject good counsel and rush headlong into a situation in which they kill two defenseless Calormenes. ("They were too angry to think clearly," comments Lewis, "But much evil came of their rashness in the end"—II.20.) Immediately after the killing, Tirian, who is good and noble at heart, recognizes that his act, though brave in the purely physical sense, was both cowardly and dishonorable—rather like Moses' rash killing of the Egyptian whom he saw beating an Israelite—and he surrenders himself to the Calormenes. Through this act of repentance, Tirian is strengthened and restored, and, like Faramir, he learns that endurance is the better part of fortitude.

In the days that follow, Tirian stands firm against the enemy, testifying boldly, and at the risk of his own martyrdom, to his faith in Aslan. (Boromir likewise repents of his cowardly and ignoble deed and is restored in the eyes of Aragorn, but his subsequent death robs him of the chance to reestablish himself as a truly courageous warrior.) Tirian's death is brought about by a second "rash" act, but one that is motivated by insight rather than impulse, duty rather than pride. In a burst of pure self-sacrifice, he grabs hold of the Calormene leader and leaps together with him into the Stable Door: a threshold that is not only fraught with physical danger but with that very numinous fear that the restored Moses felt as he stood, trembling, before the burning bush.

JOINING THE DANCE

Just as the classical virtue of courage dwells in the middle space between cowardice and rashness, so does temperance (for Aristotle) dwell midway between self-indulgence and insensitivity. That is to say, true temperance (or self-control) manifests itself neither in gluttony nor asceticism, neither in a hot prodigality nor a dry Puritanism. To deny and mortify the appetites is as intemperate as to overindulge them. Indeed, the former may be even worse than the latter, for we find in the gospels that it is the abstinent Pharisees who are more apt to reject Christ than the carousing prostitutes and tax collectors. In *The Lord of the Rings* and the Chronicles of Narnia, Tolkien and Lewis present us with characters who both avoid and embrace these two extremes.

As is well known, though Lewis and Tolkien were both orthodox Christians who took their faith seriously, neither of them was "puritanical" in his personal behavior or attitude toward others. Indeed, Jack and Tollers (as they called each other) could drink and smoke and joke with the best of them. Though neither was an alcoholic, and though both were highly disciplined in their prayers and churchgoing, they rejected outright the notion that a Christian must refrain from all fleshly pleasures as a sign of purity and devotion—an attitude that has bewildered their evangelical fans, who are legion. And this shared attitude found its way into the fictional worlds they fashioned. Thus, Tolkien's central heroes (the Hobbits) are not only big eaters and drinkers but are quite fond of pipe-weed: an "addiction" they share with the wise and "saintly" Gandalf. And Gandalf, though he can be as serious and grave as a desert monk, is filled with a life and a gaiety that is infectious. As he and Pippin stand in an upper room of Minis Tirith (the White Tower of Gondor) and prepare for the coming attack of Mordor, Gandalf suddenly lets loose a tremendous laugh that startles the Hobbit:

> Pippin glanced in some wonder at the face now close beside his own, for the sound of that laugh had been gay and merry. Yet in the wizard's face he saw at first only lines of care and sorrow;

though as he looked more intently he perceived that under all there was a great joy: a fountain of mirth enough to set a king-dom laughing, were it to gush forth. (V.i.742)

In contrast to more legalistic Christians who might consider it unseemly to laugh on the Sabbath, Gandalf (like Tolkien and Lewis) knows that Life and Joy dwell inseparably together and that those who would stem the flow of either are more likely to proceed from the camp of the enemy. Sauron knows nothing of such laughter; it is as foreign to him as goodness or light.

In *The Lion, the Witch and the Wardrobe*, Lewis makes it clear that his enemy (the White Witch) is equally devoid of all life, all joy, and all sensual pleasure. When the novel opens, we learn that the Witch has held Narnia in a perpetual Winter that never gives way to the joy, feasting, and conviviality of Christmas. With the com-ing of Aslan, however, the Witch's long Winter begins to break, and Father Christmas returns to Narnia bearing bounteous gifts of food and wine. In response, a small party of woodland animals sets up a table in the woods and begins to feast in a style not seen in Narnia for decades. Alas for these innocent revelers, their festivi-ties are interrupted by the arrival of the White Witch who, when she sees them partaking of rich food and wine, cries out in anger:

What is the meaning of all this gluttony, this waste, this self-indulgence. Where did you get all these things? (XI.112)

And when the animals respond that they were gifts of Father Christmas, the Witch, in a fit of "puritanical" rage, turns them all into statues of stone. The Witch's conception of what Narnia should be like is similar to what Sauron desires for Middle-earth (and what Satan desires for our own world): a barren landscape devoid of life peopled by joyless automatons who neither laugh nor take pleasure in anything. It is Satan, not Christ, who is the cosmic killjoy.

In *Prince Caspian*, Lewis further develops his "anti-puritanical" (but "pro-Christian") stance by rather shockingly allowing Aslan to work in tandem with Bacchus, the Greek god of wine, women, and song, to free Narnia from the tyrannical rule of the Telmarines (a race of humans who have driven the talking animals underground and silenced the trees and the rivers). It is Bacchus's fecundity and vitality, symbolized in the vine and the grape, that shatter the artificial and finally inhuman rigidity of the Telmarines. Just as Christ began His ministry by transforming water into wine at a wedding in Cana of Galilee (John 2), so the restoration of Narnia begins with an overflow of Bacchic energy that cannot be contained in the dried-up wineskins of the Telmarine usurpers.

As for the Narnians who aid Aslan and Bacchus in this restoration, they too must learn to embrace and be rejuvenated by the thunderous joy that flows from Aslan. Within the Narnian camp, Lewis places two cynical Dwarfs (Trumpkin and Nikabrik), both of whom begin as skeptics who place little hope in the old stories of Aslan. As the novel unfolds, however, Trumpkin slowly opens his mind and heart to the abundant life of Aslan while Nikabrik closes his to all that is healthy, natural, and joyous. Though the dual change that takes place in Trumpkin and Nikabrik takes many chapters to develop, Lewis prepares us for their diverse paths by noting two differences in their behavior. First, whereas Trumpkin smokes, Nikabrik does not. Second, whereas Trumpkin is willing to be touched by simple pleasures, Nikabrik refuses to be "infiltrated" by such vulgarities. This second difference is highlighted one evening when the talking animals, led by Prince Caspian, hold a festival in the forest and the fauns begin a raucous, ener-

getic dance. "Before he knew what he was doing," writes Lewis,
Caspian

> found himself joining in the dance. Trumpkin, with heavier and
> jerkier movements, did likewise and even Trufflehunter [the
> badger] hopped and lumbered about as best he could. Only
> Nikabrik stayed where he was, looking on in silence. (VI.78)

Trumpkin is a leaden dancer at best, with two left feet and no
rhythm, but at least he attempts to participate in the festivities.
Nikabrik, in his refusal to join in the dance, betrays an insensitivity to life and joy—an excess of temperance, to use Aristotle's
terminology—that parallels that of the White Witch and of the
Telmarines he is purportedly helping Caspian to overthrow.

It may—indeed, it *should*—seem strange to many Christian
readers (especially nonsmoking, teetotaling evangelicals like myself) that the "bad guy" would be the one who *refuses* to smoke or
dance, but Lewis (like Tolkien) understood that the ability and
willingness to accept and take joy in appropriate pleasures is a
virtue. If I may speak more personally for a moment, what Tolkien
and Lewis have taught me—someone who does not even drink
coffee because he refuses to be "controlled" by caffeine—is that
the true distinguishing mark between a good and bad use of alco-
hol or tobacco is whether the use of it increases or destroys love,
joy, and peace. Drunk in moderation at a wedding or smoked
moderately by a circle of friends, wine and tobacco can enhance
fellowship, inspire gratitude, and draw shy people out of themselves. Drunk or smoked in excess or in isolation for the purpose
of dulling pain, inducing stupor, or separating oneself from one's
responsibilities, they become tools of the Enemy for devouring
our personhood and robbing us of our God-given potential.

THE VIRTUE OF FARAMIR

But, of course, the temperate man is not primarily known by his tobacco. He is known most perfectly by his willingness to show restraint when the situation calls for it. He will partake of the joys of the table or the pipe when it is right and proper to do so, but he will just as quickly refuse to indulge himself when the pleasure at hand is neither right nor proper. In *The Lord of the Rings*, the character who perhaps embodies this virtue in its purest form is Faramir. Though he has always been looked down upon and even scorned by his father (Denethor) as being weaker and less manly than his warrior brother (Boromir), Faramir, in an act of classical temperance, lets pass by an opportunity to raise himself above Boromir in his father's esteem.

As Frodo and Sam make their way to Mordor, they fall in (providentially) with Faramir and his hidden band of Rangers. Faramir, who shares the discerning powers of both Denethor and Gandalf, quickly realizes that Frodo not only holds in his possession the Ring of Power but that Boromir had tried unsuccessfully (and fatally) to steal it from the Ring-bearer. If he wishes, Faramir can now do what his brother was unable to do, for Frodo and Sam are at his mercy and would be unable to resist him. Faramir knows exactly what the stakes are:

> The One Ring that was thought to have perished from the world. And Boromir tried to take it by force? And you escaped? And ran all the way—to me! And here in the wild I have you: two halflings, and a host of men at my call, and the Ring of Rings. A pretty stroke of fortune! A chance for Faramir, Captain of Gondor, to show his quality! Ha! (IV.v.665)

Yes, a chance to show his quality, and more than that: a chance to prove to his father that his strength is greater than that of his dead brother. And why should Faramir not take it? Does it not seem that all has conspired in such a way as to place the Ring in his grasp, to deliver it to him without his even asking for it?

But the temptation departs as quickly as it comes. Faramir first laughs (as Gandalf might) and then becomes grave. He knows now how sore the trial must have been for his brother, and grieves that the noble Boromir, whom he loves despite the unjust favoritism of Denethor, should have been overtaken by greed and self-indulgence. Faramir will not make the same mistake, for he knows that "there are some perils from which a man must flee" (IV.v.666). Part of the virtue of temperance consists in knowing one's limits and refusing to exceed them. He will not take the Ring; indeed, he asserts, he would not take it if he were to find it lying on the road. In this, Faramir the mortal man approaches the exemplary virtue of the High Elf Galadriel and the great wizard Gandalf, both of whom refuse the Ring when Frodo offers it to them.

First John sums up concisely the full range of human sin in three deft phrases: the lust of the flesh, the lust of the eyes, the pride of life (2:16). In refusing the Ring, Faramir rejects all three temptations and embraces instead the fullness of the virtue of temperance.

the WISDOM *that* DISCERNS

According to the Bible, Solomon was the wisest man who ever lived. But in what did his wisdom consist? When considered from our own modern perspective, Solomon qualifies as neither a brain surgeon nor a rocket scientist. He did not uncover the laws of nature or invent labor-saving gadgets or even produce any great works of art. He commissioned the Temple, but did not draw up the blueprints or ascertain the secret techniques used by the Egyptians to build the pyramids. And yet the Bible, along with the fuller Judeo-Christian tradition, insists that, of all men, he was the wisest.

What exactly did this man have who ruled Israel's greatest kingdom, spoke three thousand proverbs, wrote poetic meditations on the joys of love and the futility of life, and attracted the respect and awe of such distant monarchs as the Queen of Sheba?

What he had, in a word, was discernment: the ability to perceive and weigh the subtle distinctions between good and evil, virtue and vice, discretion and folly. His wisdom, that is to say, combined insight, intelligence, and righteousness with plain common sense. His proverbs are less metaphysical than they are pragmatic, and yet they reveal a deep understanding of the nature of God, the nature of man, the nature of the universe, and the proper interplay between the three. The polar opposite of the wise Solomon is a figure whom the book of Proverbs refers to simply and scornfully as the fool.

A FOOL'S PRISON

In the final analysis, all the "villains" in *The Lord of the Rings*—from Sauron and Saruman, to Wormtongue and Gollum, to Boromir and Denethor—are fools: not because they are stupid or even ignorant, but because they lack, to a greater or lesser degree, the virtue of discernment. Saruman, especially, deserves the biblical reproof of fool, for he is a wizard who was once gifted with vast stores of wisdom but who foolishly and contemptuously squandered them. When Gandalf the Grey learns that Bilbo's ring is the Ring of Power, he first counsels Frodo to leave the Shire and then goes himself to Isengard to seek the counsel of the head of his order, Saruman the White. When he arrives, he learns to his horror that Saruman has been corrupted by his desire for the Ring and that he now refers to himself as Saruman of Many Colors. Gandalf responds that he liked white better, to which Saruman replies:

> "White!" he sneered. "It serves as a beginning. White cloth may be dyed. The white page can be overwritten; and the white light can be broken."

"In which case it is no longer white," said I. "And he that breaks a thing to find out what it is has left the path of wisdom." (II.ii.252)

Writing in England in the 1790s, at the start of the Industrial Revolution and in the heyday of Enlightenment rationalism, the Romantic poet William Wordsworth issued a rebuke to his countrymen that is not far removed from Gandalf's rebuke of Saruman: "Sweet is the lore which Nature brings; / Our meddling intellect, / Mis-shapes the beauteous forms of things: / We murder to dissect." Discernment, though it works through the making of distinctions, does not therefore break and dissect that which it studies. It seeks fusion, wholeness, simplicity.

In the writings of Solomon, wisdom (*sophia* in Greek) is often depicted in the guise of a beautiful woman who is to be sought passionately by the philosopher (the "lover of sophia"). Wisdom is not a thing to be handled roughly or bartered for power or wealth; it is to be embraced, caressed, loved. Saruman, in his lust for power, breaks apart the pure white light of truth as a biologist might dissect a cat or dog. By so doing, he sacrifices both his own integrity and his ability to perceive simple, straightforward truth. Thus, although Saruman knows full well that there can be only one Lord of the Rings, and that, in any case, Sauron does not share power, he fools himself into believing that he can control and manipulate the Ring. His subtlety blinds him from clarity; his "deconstruction" of Truth into a thousand different shades of truth renders him incapable not only of perceiving higher moral-ethical standards, but of heeding plain, down-to-earth common sense.

In part 4 I will have much more to say about the nature of evil and its power to corrupt; here, let it suffice to say that when Saruman abandons the path of wisdom for the road to folly, he sacrifices the very ability to discern *between* wisdom and folly. Thus, after Isengard is destroyed and his forces scattered, Saruman persists in his refusal to accept the mercy of Gandalf and join in the fight against Sauron. He continues to believe that Gandalf is the fool, when it is in fact he, Saruman, who has become the fool. In the end, he so misjudges his slave and stooge (Wormtongue) that he has no time to ward off the blow when Wormtongue mortally stabs him with a hidden knife.

Saruman is, in many ways, like a group of Narnian Dwarfs who, near the end of *The Last Battle*, find themselves, along with Tirian (the last king of Narnia) and the earth children, on the other side of the Stable Door. As the Door marks the threshold between life and death, all those within the Stable now reside in what we who live on this side of the Door call the "afterlife." However, though they all occupy the same "space," what they experience in that space is vastly different. Whereas Tirian and the children find themselves in a garden of ravishing beauty and dazzling light, the Dwarfs think that they are in a "pitch-black, poky, smelly little hole of a stable" (XIII.144). They cannot see the light, for their overly subtle, Saruman-like minds have so dissected the pure light that it has been shattered into a thousand fragments and consumed by darkness.

Their loss of all wisdom-discernment begins earlier in the novel when King Tirian frees them from a chain gang and reveals to them that they have been fooled into their captivity by a donkey in a lion's skin who has pretended to be Aslan. Unfortunately, when they learn the truth about the false Aslan, they do not seek harder to know and serve the true one, but decide that they will instead reject all belief in Aslan. Just as an immature Christian who is "burned" by a phony televangelist will often react by abandoning the faith altogether, so do the Dwarfs make the illogical leap from the empirical fact of one bad "believer" to the unfounded proposition that all therefore are liars and hypocrites. Swearing that they will never be fooled again, they decide to live by a new motto:

> I don't think we want any more kings—if you *are* Tirian, which you don't look like him—no more than we want any Aslans. We're going to look after ourselves from now on and touch our caps to nobody. . . . We're on our own now. No more Aslan, no more kings, no more silly stories about other worlds. The Dwarfs are for the Dwarfs. (VII.73)

Spurred on by bitterness, ingratitude, and a "looking out for number one" philosophy, the Dwarfs lose their ability (as does Saruman) to distinguish between good and evil, virtue and vice, discretion and folly. Indeed, so fully do they lose their moral compass that in the final battle against the Calormenes, they turn traitors—*irrational* traitors—and shoot down with arrows the Narnian horses who are the last line of defense against the enemy.

And that brings us back to the Stable where the Dwarfs sit huddled in a corner, wholly unaware of the beauty and light around them. Aslan appears and lays out before them a magnificent feast of food and wine, but when they eat and drink it, it tastes to them like old hay and dirty water. Even the golden voice of Aslan sounds to them like the grating of a machine. The children are amazed and confused by the irrational behavior of the Dwarfs, but Aslan explains to them what is happening:

> They will not let us help them. They have chosen cunning instead of belief. Their prison is only in their own minds, yet they are in that prison; and so afraid of being taken in that they can not be taken out. (XIII.148)

The fools who populate the pages of *The Lord of the Rings*, the Chronicles of Narnia, and the book of Proverbs earn their name not because they lack knowledge (information) but because they lack discernment (the capacity for sifting and judging that information). In the case of the Dwarfs, it is their cunning, their refusal to be "taken in," that keeps them from perceiving and receiving the pure white light of truth and life. The prison in which they dwell is a prison of their own making, yet it is a prison nonetheless. That is not to say, as Lewis makes clear in the remaining chapters and even more forcefully in *The Great Divorce*, that heaven and hell, virtue and vice, are merely states of mind. It is to say, rather, that true wisdom is directly linked to true reality, while folly represents a shrinking and shriveling of both wisdom and reality. The fall from wisdom is ever and always a fall into darkness, confusion, and waylessness. That is why, apart from the virtue of wisdom, we cannot keep our feet on the true Road.

SEEING THROUGH THE PALANTÍRI

I said a moment ago that it is wisdom that allows us to sift and judge information properly. But part of that judging includes discerning which information we should accept and act upon. As their stay at Lórien draws to a close, Sam and Frodo are invited by Galadriel to gaze into her Mirror: a pool that reveals to those who stare into it things from the past, the present, and the future. Though one might expect that such a pool would represent a pure boon to those who seek after wisdom, Galadriel warns the Hobbits of the dangers that attend looking into the pool:

> The Mirror is dangerous as a guide of deeds. . . . You may learn
> something, and whether what you see be fair or evil, that may
> be profitable, and yet it may not. Seeing is both good and peril-

ous. Yet I think, Frodo, that you have courage and wisdom
enough for the venture, or I would not have brought you here.
(II.vii.354)

Seeing alone will not give us wisdom; rather, only those who are
already in possession of wisdom can hope to survive the ordeal
of seeing. That is to say, we do not gain wisdom by the mere accumulation of knowledge—even and especially if that knowledge
is hidden or forbidden—any more than we become a great moun-
tain climber by attempting, untrained and untested, to scale the
heights of Mt. Everest. Like the virtue of courage, wisdom calls
for great patience; it is easily destroyed and led astray by rashness.

Indeed, Saruman's loss of wisdom is caused in great part by his
rash desire to gain a knowledge that is greater than his powers of
discernment. For Saruman, as we (and Gandalf) learn later in the
book, is in possession of one of the seven palantíri, magic stones—
"crystal balls," if you will—that allow the possessor to see what
is happening across Middle-earth and beyond. The stones were
originally made for good, to help the Númenoreans (see chapter 4) to communicate with each other when they set up their
kingdoms in Middle-earth, but they eventually were corrupted
by Sauron and used by him to control the minds of those who
gazed into them. Saruman, in his folly, thinks that he is stronger
than Sauron and that he can use the knowledge gained from the
palantír to further his own designs to capture the Ring and rule
Middle-earth. But he is too weak. As Gandalf explains to Pippin:

> [T]here is nothing that Sauron cannot turn to evil uses. Alas
> for Saruman! [The palantír] was his downfall, as I now per-
> ceive. Perilous to us all are the devices of an art deeper than we
> possess ourselves. Yet he must bear the blame. Fool! to keep it
> secret for his own profit. (III.XI.583)

Fool is just the right word! Like Job, Saruman has sought a knowledge that is too "wonderful" for him (42:3), one that shatters his discernment and confuses both his intellectual and moral capacities. And this confusion does not occur because Sauron shows Saruman false images in the stone (all that is seen in the stone is true), but because he only shows him those images that he wants Saruman to see. In the absence of those sifting and judging powers that wisdom alone can give, Saruman pieces together the information improperly, as Sauron encourages him to do, and the result is that he is driven further into folly.

In the same way, Denethor, the Steward of Gondor, is corrupted by his own secret use of another palantír. Without the virtue of wisdom to direct and inform his gaze, Denethor is also encouraged by Sauron to misread and misinterpret what he sees in the stone. As a result, Denethor, believing that the West is lost and that the rule of Men is soon to be ended, falls into utter folly and despair and throws himself upon a pyre — almost incinerating Faramir with him, for his discernment has been so impaired that he cannot tell that life still remains in his son. Although Gandalf does not know until after Denethor's death of his possession of a palantír, he speaks sage words at the Council of Elrond — shortly before the setting forth of the Fellowship — that shows that he recognizes fully the specific type of danger that can be wrought by a palantír. In answer to one who claims that the Council's decision to cast the Ring into Mount Doom is motivated by folly and despair, Gandalf responds:

> It is not despair, for despair is only for those who see the end
> beyond all doubt. We do not. It is wisdom to recognize neces-
> sity, when all other courses have been weighed, though as folly
> it may appear to those who cling to false hope. (II.ii.262)

Denethor, of course, *does* see the end, at least the end Sauron wishes him to see, and it is precisely this vision that causes him to despair, to reject all hope (false or otherwise), and to cease that weighing that lies, of necessity, at the heart of wisdom.

Seeing is always perilous, but it is most perilous for those who look without wisdom.

the JUSTICE
of the KING

According to Article I, Section 9 of the US Constitution,

> No Title of Nobility shall be granted by the United States: And
> no Person holding any Office of Profit or Trust under them,
> shall, without the Consent of the Congress, accept of any pres-
> ent, Emolument, Office, or Title, of any kind whatever, from
> any King, Prince, or foreign State.

Alexander Hamilton, commenting on this clause in #84 of *The
Federalist Papers*, asserts that "the prohibition of titles of nobility . . .
may truly be denominated the cornerstone of republican government; for so long as they are excluded there can never be serious
danger that the government will be any other than that of the
people." In these two statements, which embody the very spirit of

the Founding Fathers of the American republic, we encounter an ethos, a paradigm, a worldview that is strongly at odds with that of medieval Europe, Narnia, and Middle-earth alike.

If there is one aspect of "Old Europe" that most Americans (whether they be low-church Baptists or high-church Episcopalians) have a hard time accepting, and an even harder time understanding, it is the premodern notion of hierarchy. Even American Catholics, who attend a church that is strongly hierarchical—the word means literally "rule by a high priest or a sacred person"—tend to have a natural antipathy to the concept. And that is a sad thing, for if we cannot grasp the notion of hierarchy, if we can see in it only oppression and tyranny, then our understanding of justice will be limited at best and we will find it difficult to enter, sympathetically and imaginatively, into the worlds of Narnia and Middle-earth.

Though the classical virtue of justice in its fullest and most refined sense includes the notion of the intrinsic value and dignity of all people, it is not therefore equivalent to our modern notions of inclusivism and egalitarianism. To many moderns, justice means making everything equal, everything fair, everything the same. For Plato, justice is more a balancing act between different parts of society and of the soul. Justice is embodied in the state, not when all roles, classes, and distinctions are collapsed, but when each performs his or her role properly, faithfully, and in harmony. The same goes, I would argue, for the body of Christ, which is made up of many members that operate in harmony: members that possess equal worth but are not therefore equally interchangeable (see 1 Corinthians 12). In the more distinctly Christian notion of justice, a new element is added—or, better, highlighted, since it is not wholly absent from the writings and practices of what Dante calls the "virtuous pagans." That notion is humility, and it manifests itself in the concept of the leader as steward.

Perhaps the crowning example of stewardship in the premodern world is that of Jesus washing the feet of His disciples (John 13). Many in our antihierarchical age would like to read this famous episode as proof that Jesus was an egalitarian, that He advocated the collapsing of roles and the ending of all distinction between master and servant. This is not the case! If we read the passage carefully, we will note that the foot washing is framed by two statements: "Jesus knew that the Father had put all things under his power, and that he had come from God and was returning to God" (verse 3 NIV); "I tell you the truth, no servant is greater than his master, nor is a messenger greater than the one who sent him" (verse 16 NIV). Jesus' act of humility, these verses make clear, is performed out of a position of strength and full self-knowledge of who He is as Son of God and Lord. If Jesus had wanted to advocate a full collapsing of roles and full egalitarianism, verse 16 would have announced the end of the distinction between master and servant, but it does not. Indeed, the humility (and justice) of Jesus' act only has meaning inasmuch as He *is* the master and those whose feet He washes *are* His servants. Apart from a clear sense of hierarchy, stewardship and humility have no meaning.

THE KING'S REDEMPTIVE RULE

Neither in medieval Europe nor in the lands of Narnia and Middle-earth do the good subjects look upon their king as divine. To speak of the "divine right" of kings is not to claim that the king is a god on earth — as he was, say, for the ancient Egyptians or the premodern Japanese — but to assert that his authority ultimately proceeds from God, the King of Heaven. The king, when he is most worthy of himself and his office, not only dispenses but *makes* justice. That is to say, his office is not fully realized if all he does is enforce the laws, protect the realm, and issue judgments from his throne. He must also, in a fuller sense, set things right—restore and reorient that which has become diseased or unbalanced within the body politic.

When, near the end of *The Lord of the Rings*, Gandalf and the Hobbits stop for the night at Bree and visit with Barliman Butterbur, the proprietor of the Prancing Pony, Gandalf explains to him what it means that Aragorn the king has returned to Gondor and taken up his crown:

> [T]here is a king again, Barliman. He will soon be turning his mind this way. Then the Greenway will be opened again, and his messengers will come north, and there will be comings and goings, and the evil things will be driven out of the waste-lands. Indeed the waste in time will be waste no longer, and there will be people and fields where once there was wilderness. (VI. vii.971)

Like the mythical Theseus, king of Athens, and the legendary Arthur, king of Britain, Aragorn, king of Gondor, begins his reign by cleaning up the roads: an action that both asserts his royal power and authority and extends and embodies his royal justice. He is doing more than allowing for the safe passage of travelers and merchants; he is enabling fecundity to take root where there was once only wilderness. The king, as minister of justice, drives out evil from the waste places, and it is significant that Gandalf says this exorcism of the land will take place, not when the king rides in state to Bree, but when he *turns his mind* in that direction. The virtue of justice is an inherently creative one; it recalls the six-day creation week of Genesis 1 during which God brought shape and order to the primal chaos through the speaking of words. Now that King Aragorn has come again to dwell in his city, he will bring harmony to its several parts in a way directly analogous to how justice brings harmony to the various warring parts of our soul (in Plato's *Republic*) or to how Christ, when He reigns as Lord of our heart, brings harmony to the various warring parts of our fallen and recalcitrant will.

If I seem here to be speaking of the return of King Aragorn in language that is almost messianic, that is only because Tolkien does so himself. Consider the third stanza of the song that the Eagle sings, proclaiming Aragorn's imminent return: "Sing and be glad, all ye children of the West, / for your King shall come again, / and he shall dwell among you / all the days of your life" (VI.v.942). Tolkien's language here, and throughout book VI, chapter V, skillfully incorporates the prophetic rhetoric and imagery that the Bible uses to proclaim the second coming of the Christ and His great marriage to the church (His Bride), an event that will signal the end of the Old Age and the beginning of the New:

> And I saw a new heaven and a new earth: for the first heaven and the first earth were passed away; and there was no more sea. And I John saw the holy city, new Jerusalem, coming down from God out of heaven, prepared as a bride adorned for her husband. And I heard a great voice out of heaven saying, Behold, the tabernacle of God is with men, and he will dwell with them, and they shall be his people, and God himself shall be with them, and be their God. (Revelation 21:1–3)

The crowning of Aragorn and his royal marriage to Arwen (the half-elven daughter of Elrond) effect a double union that brings all to completion, all to harmony, all to perfection:

> And Gandalf said [to Aragorn]: "This is your realm and the heart of the greater realm that shall be. The Third Age of the world is ended, and the new age is begun; and it is your task to order its beginning and to preserve what may be preserved. (Vi.v.949)

It is this greater sense of order and preservation, of consummation and fulfillment, that is missing from our modern understanding of justice. Too often, justice is reduced to making sure that everyone gets exactly the same piece of pie and is treated in exactly the same way; or, even worse, that everyone gets his "day in court": not so that his deeds may be judged but so that he can, if he has a good enough attorney, eliminate all risk and responsibility from his life.

Praise be to God that a day is coming when all things on heaven and earth will be brought to judgment before the messianic King. On that final dawn Christ will set all things to right and true justice, not envy-driven fairness, will reign. For those who oppose His will, it will be a day of wrath, but for those who make up the Bride of Christ, it will mark the beginning of eternal joy.

KINGS AND QUEENS OF NARNIA

Though Narnia is far more a "fairy land" than Middle-earth, it too runs best when there is a strong and legitimate king on the throne. Narnia, when it is not controlled by a tyrant like the White Witch, is a place of freedom, and yet, it is also a place of order and hierarchy. Shortly after Aslan creates Narnia and gives the gift of speech to a chosen number of animals, he announces the tragic news that evil has already entered Narnia in the form of the evil Queen Jadis (who will eventually become the White Witch). Aslan, however, does not abandon his new world to the devices of Jadis. Rather, he sets in motion two remedies to stem the spread of evil and guard his beloved Narnians. The first of these remedies involves crowning a human, a Son of Adam, to be the first king of Narnia. This seems an odd thing to do, and even "unfair," since Narnia belongs not to Men but to Talking Animals. But Aslan decrees it nonetheless. He then gives this charge to his first king and queen (Frank and Helen):

> You shall rule and name all these creatures, and do justice among them, and protect them from their enemies when enemies arise. And enemies will arise, for there is an evil Witch in this world. (*The Magician's Nephew*, XI.138)

Though Frank is only a humble cabby, Aslan raises him up to be a king and the father of a line of kings. Still, Frank is to retain his humility and his servant's heart: he is to work the earth with spade and plough, to rule the Talking Animals with kindness, to be the first in battle and the last in retreat, and to be careful that he does not play favorites among his children or his subjects. He is not to rule for his own pleasure or profit, but to keep the peace in Narnia.

This he does, and the justice of his reign and that of his descendants is not forgotten by those Talking Animals who are loyal and true subjects. Indeed, when, many thousands of years later, Narnia is seized by the tyrannical Telmarines (who are humans) and the Talking Animals are driven underground (in *Prince Caspian*), those who are most loyal and true retain their allegiance to Aslan's original decree. Thus, when good Prince Caspian (nephew to the cruel usurper, Miraz) flees into the forest for safety, he is greeted kindly by the Talking Animals, who want him to be their king, even though he is related to the despotic Miraz. One of the Dwarfs, however, does not feel so kindly toward Caspian—he is, after all, a human, and the last several human "administrations" have not treated either the Dwarfs or the beasts kindly. But Trufflehunter the Badger will have nothing to do with such treasonous talk:

> You Dwarfs are as forgetful and changeable as the Humans themselves. I'm a beast, I am, and a Badger what's more. We don't change. We hold on. I say great good will come of it. This is the true King of Narnia we've got here: a true King coming back to true Narnia. And we beasts remember, even if Dwarfs forget, that Narnia was never right except when a Son of Adam was King. (V.65)

Rightness is as good a synonym as any for the classical virtue of justice. It is right, proper, and natural that a Son of Adam should rule over the beasts. This hierarchical situation does not diminish the beasts, nor does it rob them of dignity, value, or "self-esteem"; on the contrary, it allows them to be exactly who and what they are. In the same way, Sam's position as Frodo's servant does not prevent but enables him to be the wise and courageous hero that he is.

I said above that without a full understanding of hierarchy we will have a hard time sympathizing with *The Lord of the Rings*, and yet there exist millions of "antihierarchical" readers whose love for Middle-earth is as strong as their aversion to anything that smacks of "elitism." How can this be? I would suggest the following "solution" for this odd disparity between the often "rebel" nature of Tolkien's fans and the pro-monarchical stance of his epic:

such fans are drawn to the work precisely because it embodies a sense of rightness, of justice, of nobility that they sense is lacking in themselves and in their culture.

No matter how strongly the modern world (and our own Constitution!) has conditioned us to resist all titles and forms of nobility, nothing can prevent that sense of rightness that falls on most readers when they reach the end of the epic and witness the crowning of Aragorn. And that sense of rightness, of proportion, of "fittedness" is inseparable from the virtue of justice. It is all tied up with that moment of awe and consummation that we experience when we read of the final transformation of the dusty, disheveled, weary Strider into the glorious King Aragorn:

> But when Aragorn arose all that beheld him gazed in silence, for it seemed to them that he was revealed to them now for the first time. Tall as the sea-kings of old, he stood above all that were near; ancient of days he seemed and yet in the flower of manhood; and wisdom sat upon his brow, and strength and healing were in his hands, and a light was about him. (VI.v.947)

PART THREE

The Theological Virtues

CHAPTER NINE

REHABILITATING
FRIENDSHIP

C. S. Lewis and J. R. R. Tolkien were far more than good friends. In addition to their long years of fellowship and camaraderie, the two professors were, for lack of a better phrase, apologists for friendship. Though friendship appears neither on the fourfold list of classical virtues nor on the threefold list of theological virtues, Lewis and Tolkien, in both their lives and their writings, sought to revive and rehabilitate friendship as a virtue worthy of respect. Indeed, in *The Four Loves*, Lewis devotes a chapter to the subject in which he vigorously defends it as a type of love which, though it may have no "survival value," lends "value to survival." (The other three loves Lewis discusses are *eros* or physical love, affection, and *agape* or self-giving love.) "To the Ancients," writes Lewis in the first paragraph of chapter IV, "Friendship seemed the happiest and most fully human of all loves; the crown of life and the school of virtue. The modern world, in comparison, ignores it." While Romanticism, Lewis explains, exalted sentiment, thus strengthening and raising the reputation of affection, and Freudianism exalted instinct, thus raising the reputation of eros, friendship was dismissed as unnecessary at best (it is not required for survival or procreation) and elitist at worst (it undemocratically separates us from others who are not part of our group). But it was not always so. In ancient and medieval times, argues Lewis,

> Affection and Eros were [considered] too obviously connected with our nerves, too obviously shared with the brutes. You could feel these tugging at your guts and fluttering in your diaphragm. But in Friendship—in that luminous, tranquil, rational world of relationships freely chosen—you got away from all that. This alone, of all the loves, seemed to raise you to the level of gods or angels.

Odd as it may sound to modern ears, Lewis and Tolkien viewed friendship as an almost spiritual thing, something that transcended the physical without abandoning it, and they were both active in forming groups where they could gather with like-minded friends for fellowship.

The most important of those societies was a group known as the Inklings, which Lewis and Tolkien began in 1933 and that carried on throughout World War II and beyond. The purpose of the group (which included Charles Williams, Owen Barfield, and Lewis's brother, Warren) was to allow an open forum where members could discuss various topics and could read aloud their own works in progress. It was at such meetings that Tolkien read his early drafts of *The Lord of the Rings* and received the enthusiastic support and encouragement of his peers, especially Lewis. In the midst of a surrounding society that held a particularly low opinion of the kind of "escapist" literature that Tolkien and Lewis so loved, the Inklings provided the two writers with a nurturing space where they could spin their fantastical tales. Not surprisingly, the friendship of the Inklings—exactly the kind of friendship for which Lewis and Tolkien were apologists—proved to be one of the main resources of strength that invigorated them in their attempts to rehabilitate the genres of epic romance and the fairy tale: genres for which they were apologists as well.

FRIENDSHIP AND THE FELLOWSHIP

Whereas the narrative structures of the seven separate Chronicles of Narnia, focused as they are on child heroes, did not allow Lewis the proper scope to explore the type of mature and multi-faceted friendship that he and Tolkien found in the Inklings, *The Lord of the Rings* proved an ideal vehicle for sounding the full depth of the "virtue" of friendship: a subject to which Aristotle devotes two full books of his *Nicomachean Ethics*—almost as much as he devotes to the four classical virtues combined! At the very core of Tolkien's epic lie a series of friendships that are themselves gathered together into the wider Fellowship of the nine. Indeed, it is these friendships, more than anything else, that enable the Fellowship to fulfill its mission. When Elrond appoints the nine walkers at Rivendell, he initially leaves Pippin and Merry out of the count, but when they insist on being included, Gandalf persuades Elrond to allow it. His reason: their friendship is itself a type of strength that may prove, in the end, more powerful than the might of Men or the wisdom of the Elves. Like the light in Galadriel's phial, which she promises Frodo will shine for him in dark places, the friendship of the Hobbits is a power that endures when courage runs out, that holds firm when all the other virtues have been expended.

Frodo initially sets out from the Shire accompanied only by Sam. In fact, he takes great precaution to ensure that no other Hobbits discover his plan to flee to Rivendell. His plan, however, soon leaks out (via the talkative Sam) and is discovered by Merry and Pippin, who announce their intention to join them on their quest. At first, Frodo is upset by this turn of events, fearing that he can no longer trust anyone, but Merry soon sets his mind at rest:

> It all depends on what you want. . . . You can trust us to stick
> to you through thick and thin—to the bitter end. And you can
> trust us to keep any secret of yours—closer than you keep
> it yourself. But you cannot trust us to let you face trouble
> alone and go off without a word. We are your friends, Frodo.
> (I.v.103)

It is precisely this spirit of unswerving loyalty and devotion, this binding together of separate lives and wills, that gives the Hobbits their staying power—that makes them a fellowship, even when they are apart. At times, their friendship impels them to act in ways that are stubborn, impolite, or even borderline unethical. When Sam is chosen by Gandalf to accompany Frodo and then is later chosen by Elrond to join the Fellowship, the choosing occurs in part because he is discovered eavesdropping. The passage quoted above is itself preceded by Merry and Pippin's confession that they have long been conspiring to put Frodo in a position whereby he must agree to allow them to join him. In any other context, Sam's eavesdropping and Merry and Pippin's conspiring might be considered unacceptable, even malevolent; motivated as it is by the needs and demands of friendship, their behavior becomes acceptable, even virtuous. The good father, Jesus tells us in the Sermon on the Mount, does not give his son a stone when he asks for bread or a serpent when he asks for a fish (Matthew 7:9–10). No doubt, he would also not give his son a serpent if he asked for a serpent.

The good friend is equally committed to doing what is best for his companion—which sometimes means acting in ways that thwart the immediate desires of his companion so that his true, long-term interest might be best preserved. Thus, when Frodo is forced to break away from the Fellowship at the end of Book II (after Boromir tries to steal the Ring), Sam must force Frodo to take him along by threatening to scuttle all the boats if he does not agree. Though he knows he is being manipulated, Frodo also sees that it is Sam's loyalty and friendship that lie behind his threat. And so he laughs warmly and exclaims:

> So all my plan is spoilt! . . . It is no good trying to escape you.
> But I'm glad, Sam. I cannot tell you how glad. Come along!
> (II.x.397)

Had Sam not forced himself upon his friend at this critical moment, Frodo's journey would certainly have failed. As Frodo himself admits as they approach Shelob's lair, he would not have gotten far without Sam (IV.viii.697).

Though neither I nor Tolkien nor Lewis would ever claim that friendship is an absolute good in the name of which any act can be justified—like any other good thing in our world, friendship can too easily be corrupted into an evil cabal or a vain clique or coterie, what Lewis called an "inner ring"—the legitimate demands of friendship do often call us to break with convention. At times, they even call us to do things that might otherwise seem irrational. For example, when the Fellowship breaks, and Aragorn, Gimli, and Legolas learn that Merry and Pippin have been kidnapped by a band of Orcs, they choose not the "sensible" path of making their way to a safe refuge (like Gondor), but set out to rescue their captive friends:

> "I will follow the Orcs," [Aragorn] said at last. "I would have guided Frodo to Mordor and gone with him to the end; but if I seek him now in the wilderness, I must abandon the captives to torment and death. My heart speaks clearly at last: the fate of the Bearer is in my hands no longer. The Company has played its part. Yet we that remain cannot forsake our companions while we have strength left. Come! We will go now." (III.i.409)

When he makes this resolution, Aragorn already suspects that Sam has gone with Frodo. The greater and more pressing need is to rescue Merry and Pippin, one that must take precedence, so Aragorn asserts, over all other concerns.

E. M. Forster once famously quipped that if he had to choose between betraying his country and betraying his friends, he wished he would have the courage to betray his country. In *The Lord of the Rings*, this dilemma is revealed as a false one. If Aragorn were to abandon Merry and Pippin, he would also be abandoning all that is good and worth preserving in Middle-earth. He would, in a sense, be abdicating his own kingship. In this situation, he can best serve his country by staying true to his friends. In fact, it is at the very moment that Aragorn makes his decision to pursue the captives that he first becomes the true leader he is destined to be: for it is at this moment that his heart at last speaks clearly and the Road at last lies plain before him. "Greater love hath no man than this, that a man lay down his life for his friends" (John 15:13). If he is to become the messianic king who will bring healing and restoration to the land, Aragorn must show his willingness to sacrifice himself, not just for abstract principles but for real subjects and friends who look to him for protection.

And, as it turns out, this willingness proves contagious! Later in the book, when Aragorn realizes that he must face the terror of the Paths of the Dead, he finds that he need not face that terror alone. Gimli and Legolas choose freely to accompany him and to remain at his side no matter the danger. They do so in part because they are loyal subjects to the heir of the throne of Gondor, but they do so even more because they count Aragorn as their friend — even as they account each other as friends and dear companions. Indeed, of all the friendships in *The Lord of the Rings*, the most remarkable is the one that slowly develops between Gimli the Dwarf and Legolas the Elf. Though their races have been bitter enemies for many generations, the stubborn, feisty Dwarf and the aloof, distant Elf form a bond that promises a healing and a reconciliation that no victory on the battlefield could ever accomplish. Their equal membership in the Fellowship of the Ring helps to pull them out of their "nationalistic" pride and give them a new identity as fellow travelers on the Road. Their friendship raises them up to an almost spiritual level that transcends the petty jealousies and often irrational mistrust that have kept their people apart for thousands of years.

Of course, their bonding does not occur overnight. In the beginning they both share in the jealousies and mistrust of their races. When Gimli is told by the Elves of Lórien that he must be blindfolded lest he (a Dwarf) spy out their secrets, and Aragorn (in a beautiful act of humility and camaraderie) insists that they all be blindfolded lest Gimli be singled out and thus shamed, Legolas is indignant and does not wish to share in the humiliation of Gimli. As the two travel together, however, they come to have a deep appreciation for the gifts and insights of the other. Legolas learns to admire the bravery of the Dwarfs, while Gimli comes to appreciate the beauty of the Elves: he even pledges himself, like a chivalric knight, to serve and honor the name of the Lady Galadriel. The two fight side by side and both reach a point where they are willing to sacrifice their life for the other. But the pinnacle of their friendship, to my mind at least, is not reached on the battlefield but in a special pact they make: one they promise to fulfill when the battle has ended and peace has been restored to Middle-earth. The pact rises up out of a dialogue in which the two soldiers share a deep desire and yearning that they, as Dwarf and Elf, carry close to their heart. Gimli longs to explore the endless chambers of the Caverns of Helm's Deep, while Legolas longs with an equal ardor and passion to journey through the deep green woods of Fangorn Forest. After listening to Gimli extol the loveliness of the minerals that lie deep in the Caverns as though they were living trees, Legolas responds:

> "Almost you make me regret that I have not seen these caves. Come! Let us make this bargain—if we both return safe out of the peril that awaits us, we will journey for a while together. You shall visit Fangorn with me, and then I will come with you to see Helm's Deep."
>
> "That would not be the way of return that I should choose," said Gimli. "But I will endure Fangorn, if I have your promise to come back to the caves and share their wonder with me."
>
> "You have my promise," said Legolas. (III.viii.535)

Here, the two friends who were once enemies move beyond simply accepting each other. As with all those who possess the virtue of friendship, they wish to see the world *through* the eyes of the other, to understand and share in a passion that lies at the core of the other's being.

FRIENDSHIP IN THE CHRONICLES

I said above that The Chronicles of Narnia do not really lend themselves to a full exploration of friendship, especially of the mature kind that forms between Gimli and Legolas. Nevertheless, Lewis does present his readers with a world in which camaraderie on the Road and on the battlefield are treasured, a world where men are not embarrassed to embrace in public and where adults and children alike learn the value of Christ's call to lay down our lives for our friends. Even the two "bad boys" (Edmund in *The Lion, the Witch and the Wardrobe* and Eustace in *The Voyage of the Dawn Treader*) learn the value of friendship and self-sacrifice. In the final battle with the Witch, Edmund places himself in harm's way to protect his comrades from the Witch's wand; when Eustace is transformed into a dragon, he uses his terrible situation to assist his fellow crewmen. We even learn (in *The Last Battle*) that all the earth children from the previous six books (except one) have taken to gathering on occasion to share their memories of Narnia and their adventures with Aslan. It is their own special group: a nurturing space — like that which Lewis and Tolkien found in the Inklings — where they can indulge in a shared love for a type of beauty, mystery, and wonder for which the outside world feels only unbelief and scorn.

"Friendship," writes Lewis in *The Four Loves*, "must be about something. . . . Those who have nothing can share nothing; those who are going nowhere can have no fellow-travellers." Like the nine walkers, the friends of Narnia share both a passion and a Road.

the EYES *of* FAITH

U nlike those who study and interpret it, the Bible itself, with
its firm narrative thrust, is not overly concerned with pre-
cise definition. But there is one word for which it offers as clear
and succinct a definition as any systematic theologian could ask
for: "Now faith is the substance of things hoped for, the evidence
of things not seen" (Hebrews 11:1). Faith does not mean believing
what you know is not true, nor does it mean trusting in that which
is irrational or illogical. It means, rather, believing in what you cannot see with your physical eyes and trusting in promises that issue
from an authority in whom you have confidence. As Hebrews 11
goes on to explain by illustration, Noah had faith when he built an
enormous ark under sunny skies; Abraham had faith when he set
out for the land promised him by God (see chapter 2) and when he
believed, along with Sarah, that they would bear a child though

his wife was barren and advanced in years; Moses had faith when he forsook the riches of Egypt to suffer with his people. All trusted in promises whose fulfillment they could not see, and were willing to suffer scorn, isolation, and persecution in order to stay true to that trust. On them rested the direct call of God, and yet, far more numerous are those who trust in promises whose scope is more general. Such are those who waited patiently for the coming of the Messiah, prophesied in a hundred different ways in the Scriptures, and those who, on this side of Easter, await Christ's return.

In Greek, there are two different words for "time": the first, *chronos*, refers to simple, chronological time; the second, *kairos*, points to a temporal convergence, a critical, opportune moment when all the strands come together. For Christians, the birth of Christ in Bethlehem marked just such a *kairos*, one for which the faithful yearned and longed. Lewis himself experienced just such a *kairos* during a late night stroll he took with Tolkien. At the time, Lewis was a theist but found himself unable to accept the seemingly mythical tale of the incarnation of Christ. That is, until Tolkien suggested to him that the reason the Gospel story sounded like a myth might be because Christ was the fulfillment, not only of the Jewish prophecies, but of all the highest yearnings of the "virtuous pagans"—in short, a myth that came true. This simple but profound truth galvanized the skeptical Lewis and served as the final, culminating signpost to guide him home to his Journey's End. It was a truth that neither he nor Tolkien would forget when they constructed their epic fantasies.

KAIROS IN RIVENDELL

Like the Jews who lived at the time of Christ, the many races of Middle-earth also awaited the coming of a messiah: a savior-king who would rid the land of darkness and bring freedom and peace. In fact, when the four Hobbits arrive at Rivendell, they soon discover that they are not the only travelers who have been drawn to the hidden kingdom (and refuge) of Elrond. Others have found their way, by different roads and for different purposes, to the court of the Elven King. They all sense that a *kairos* is approaching—that the long, slow forces of history are coming to a head—but none of them can see or understand the full picture. To accomplish this piecing together of the fuller puzzle, Elrond calls for a Council, one that wends its way slowly and gracefully through the single longest chapter of the epic (book II, chapter II). One after the other, the members of the Council tell their portion of the tale and share what motivated them to seek out Rivendell.

As a Christian, I often wonder what it must have been like for the newly converted Paul as he took up his beloved Hebrew Scriptures—most of which he probably had memorized—and looked at them again with his new eyes of faith. How thrilling it must have been as all the elusive clues, all the riddling prophecies dovetailed together and a picture slowly emerged of that same Jesus of Nazareth whom he had been persecuting. It is with a similar thrill that I read Tolkien's longest chapter, marveling at how he uses it as a narrative device for gathering and synthesizing a dozen different prophecies, episodes, and personal testimonies. Tolkien even allows us, as readers, to participate in the piecing together. For most of book I, we wonder patiently why Gandalf neither returned to the Shire to assist Frodo in his flight nor met him, as he had promised, at Bree. Only now, at the Council of Elrond, does Gandalf (and Tolkien) finally reveal the sequence of events that caused him to be cut off from Frodo.

Perhaps the most exciting part of the Council, the part that is most fully and richly biblical in its scope, occurs when Boromir and Aragorn "compare notes." After sharing the tragic news that Sauron has taken back the lands around Mordor and that most of Gondor's eastern forces have been destroyed, Boromir explains his reason for coming to Rivendell:

> In this evil hour I have come on an errand over many dangerous leagues to Elrond: a hundred and ten days I have journeyed all alone. But I do not seek allies in war. The might of Elrond is in wisdom not in weapons, it is said. I come to ask for counsel and the unravelling of hard words. For on the eve of the sudden assault a dream came to my brother [Faramir] in a troubled sleep; and afterwards a like dream came oft to him again, and once to me.
>
> In that dream I thought the eastern sky grew dark and there was a growing thunder, but in the West a pale light lingered, and out of it I heard a voice, remote but clear, crying: Seek for the Sword that was broken; / In Imladris it dwells; / There shall be counsels taken / Stronger than Morgul-spells. / There shall be shown a token / That Doom is near at hand, / For Isildur's Bane shall waken, / And the Halfling forth shall stand. (II.ii.239–40)

It is, I believe, passages like this that have helped to make *The Lord of the Rings* the book of the century, one that is read and reread by millions of fans all over the world. On the simplest level, such passages provide us with the joy of discovery, that electric "aha" moment when the lightbulb flashes and a connection is forged. "Yes," we think to ourselves, "I can figure out the riddle. The broken sword is Narsil, the hilt-shard of which Isildur used to cut the Ring from Sauron's finger. And the Ring is itself Isildur's Bane, for it betrayed him, and he was killed by Orc arrows. That Ring now rests around the neck of Frodo the Hobbit (or halfling), who has, like Boromir, been drawn to Imladris (the Elvish name for Rivendell)." This joy of discovery is then multiplied threefold when we realize that the prophetic poem that speaks of Aragorn—which we have heard before at the Prancing Pony in a letter written by Gandalf, but which is now recited again with greater meaning by Bilbo—can be fitted together perfectly with the prophetic dream of Faramir. Piece by piece the face on the puzzle emerges.

However, I would argue that the deep response that such passages elicit from Tolkien's fans cannot be explained merely as a function of this thrilling "emergence"—after all, a good mystery novel provides its readers with the same thrill. Behind Boromir's testimony lurks something else that our modern world is desperately in need of: a sense that we live in a meaningful universe where nothing is accidental and where an overruling providence moves things forward in accordance with a higher plan. This promises as well that history is not merely a succession of unrelated events ("one darn thing after another"), but that it too is imbued with meaning, purpose, and direction. And if both the universe and history are meaningful, then perhaps we are as well. *The Lord of the Rings* opens our eyes to such a possibility. But if our eyes are to remain open, if we are to perceive the deeper weave, then we need something else.

We need the theological virtue of faith.

Of such faith, Boromir, unlike his brother Faramir, is sadly and tragically lacking. Although he possesses the courage to seek out the answer to the vision and though he has the wisdom to understand it, his lack of faith prevents him from trusting the very promise whose meaning he has fought so hard to find. He knows that the Ring is "Isildur's *Bane*," that it destroys all who seek to possess it, and yet he faithlessly attempts to take it from Frodo. In the end, his fate is identical to that of Isildur: he is killed by Orc arrows. But Faramir, to whom the vision first comes, retains his faith in the promise (as Sir Galahad does in his vision of the Holy Grail), and he alone of his family survives to hail the return of the king.

FAITH AND ULTIMATE MEANING

In *The Lion, the Witch and the Wardrobe*, the coming of Aslan and the defeat of the White Witch are likewise prophesied in two riddling "rhymes" that must be properly assembled. The first speaks of Aslan's return, while the second speaks of four thrones being filled by humans ("Adam's flesh and Adam's bone" in the words of the rhyme). Only in the convergence of the two seemingly unrelated prophecies can the answer be found and the *kairos* identified. Mr. Beaver, illumined by the eyes of faith, makes the connection:

> So things must be drawing near their end now he's come and
> you've come. We've heard of Aslan coming into these parts
> before—long ago, nobody can say when. But there's never been
> any of your race here before. (VIII.76–7)

Mr. Beaver, like all who possess the virtue of faith, trusts in the promises of old, and he is filled with joy when he perceives that, to paraphrase a beloved Christmas carol, the hopes and fears of all the years are finally being met together. Caspian (in *Prince Caspian*) shares Mr. Beaver's faith, even though he lives in a Narnia that has not heard of Aslan's coming for a thousand years. Still, he trusts faithfully to the old tales of Aslan and the earth children, and encouraged by his tutor, Dr. Cornelius, searches for signs of his return in the woods and the rivers and the stars.

Unfortunately, Caspian's descendant, King Tirian, suffers a lapse in faith that proves fatal in the end. When he hears that Aslan has returned to Narnia, he seeks the counsel of Roonwit the Centaur whose knowledge of the stars is like that of the magi. Roonwit warns Tirian that he has seen terrible things in the heavens:

> The stars say nothing of the coming of Aslan, nor of peace, nor of joy. I know by my art that there have not been such disastrous conjunctions of the planets for five hundred years. It was already in my mind to come and warn your Majesty that some great evil hangs over Narnia. But last night the rumour reached me that Aslan is abroad in Narnia. Sire, do not believe this tale. It cannot be. The stars never lie, but Men and Beasts do. If Aslan were really coming to Narnia, the sky would have foretold it. If he were really come, all the most gracious stars would be assembled in his honour. (*The Last Battle*, II.15)

The signs are plain, as plain as the prophecies that are spoken at the Council of Elrond, yet Tirian (like Boromir) refuses to heed them. He will do things in his own manner rather than trust the facts facing him. Like Boromir, but unlike Faramir, he lacks the faith (and the temperance, see chapter 6) to rest contented in that middle space between the issuing of the prophecies and the fulfillment of the *kairos*.

It may seem strange that I have highlighted the role of faith in *The Lord of the Rings* when, in fact, Tolkien never once mentions God by name. In many ways, Tolkien's epic sounds the same paradox as the biblical book of Esther. Although the name of God (Jehovah or Yahweh) is never uttered in Esther, it is clear that His providence watches over all that happens in the court of Xerxes the Persian. Indeed, in what is surely the best-known verse, Esther is told by the faithful (and faith-filled) Mordecai that it is up to her to intercede for her people before the king, no matter the personal cost: "And who knows but that you have come to royal position for such a time as this?" (4:14). Tolkien, I believe, echoes this verse several times in his epic.

In words that are similar both in rhetoric and import to those of Mordecai, Gandalf counsels Aragorn: "'Yet it is not our part to master all the tides of the world, but to do what is in us for the succour of those years wherein we are set, uprooting the evil in the fields that we know, so that those who live after may have clean earth to till'" (V.ix.861). At the very outset of the novel, Gandalf offers essentially the same advice to Frodo, after the frightened Hobbit shares with the wizard his wish that these things had not happened in his time:

> So do I . . . and so do all who live to see such times. But that is not for them to decide. All we have to decide is what to do with the time that is given us. (I.ii.50)

The eyes of faith are not always bright. At times they can see only dim shadows, like rough shapes reflected in a worn and dusty mirror. Yet even then, *especially* then, the faithful are called to trust in the promises of old and to believe that the time and place of their birth were no accident. For faith sees not only that history is meaningful, that it is going someplace, but also understands its own limited role *within* that history.

CHAPTER ELEVEN

HOPE *and the* HAPPY ENDING

Though *The Lord of the Rings* and The Chronicles of Narnia have thrilled, delighted, and challenged readers for half a century, and will no doubt continue to do so for centuries to come, there are still many "naysayers" who would criticize both works for being "escapist" literature: especially *The Lord of the Rings*, since its carefully detailed realism and its "pretension" to being an epic are more threatening to the modern "guardians" of high culture. Tolkien was well aware of this critique of his work—and of the work of other writers who ventured into the world of faerie—and he answers it forcefully (and wittily!) toward the end of his book-length essay "On Fairy-Stories" (in the section titled "Recovery, Escape, Consolation"):

In what the misusers are fond of calling Real Life, Escape is evidently as a rule very practical, and may even be heroic. In real life it is difficult to blame it, unless it fails; in criticism it would seem to be worse the better it succeeds. Evidently we are faced with a misuse of words, and also by a confusion of thought. Why should a man be scorned if, finding himself in prison, he tries to get out and go home? Or if, when he cannot do so, he thinks and talks about other topics than jailers and prison-walls?

Which is just another way of saying that our culture has lost the vital theological virtue of hope. Though moderns still understand, albeit in a restricted and debased way, the virtues of faith and love, they tend to dismiss hope as an immature escape from the harsh and gritty "truths" of the "real" world. Tolkien gives the lie to this notion by reminding us that the (political) prisoner who tries to escape from his cell is neither naïve nor blindly optimistic; he is, in fact, both practical and realistic. He refuses to define himself by the artificial boundaries around him and yearns for the free open air that he knows exists outside his prison walls.

If faith is more a transcendent vision, then hope is more an imminent expectation: the former gives us new eyes with which to see the unseen; the second gives us a new heart that cannot be defeated by present pain or darkness. To live in hope is to know for a certainty, to know with one's whole being, that good will come out of evil, that there will be a happy ending. And not some forced, arbitrary, tagged-on happy ending, but one that is both natural and necessary, that rises up out of the evil itself. The kind of ending that you could never have guessed but that strikes you, when it comes, as exactly the *right* kind of ending.

In the same section of "On Fairy-Stories" from which I quoted above, Tolkien identifies the "Consolation of the Happy Ending" as the central, nonnegotiable element of the fairy tale:

> Tragedy is the true form of Drama, its highest function; but the opposite is true of Fairy-story. Since we do not appear to possess a word that expresses this opposite — I will call it *Eucatastrophe*. The *eucatastrophic* tale is the true form of fairy-tale, and its highest function.
>
> The consolation of fairy-stories, the joy of the happy ending: or more correctly of the good catastrophe, the sudden joyous "turn" (for there is no true end to any fairy-tale): this joy, which is one of the things which fairy-stories can produce supremely well, is not essentially "escapist" nor "fugitive." In its fairy-tale — or otherworld — setting, it is a sudden and miraculous grace: never to be counted on to recur. It does not deny the existence of *dyscatastrophe*, of sorrow and failure: the possibility of these is necessary to the joy of deliverance; it denies (in the face of much evidence, if you will) universal final defeat and in so far is *evangelium* [good news], giving a fleeting glimpse of Joy, Joy beyond the walls of the world, poignant as grief.
>
> It is the mark of a good fairy-story, of the higher or more complete kind, that however wild its events, however fantastic or terrible the adventures, it can give to child or man that hears it, when the "turn" comes, a catch of the breath, a beat and lifting of the heart, near to (or indeed accompanied by) tears, as keen as that given by any form of literary art, and having a peculiar quality.

I quote this passage in full for it is probably the best gloss ever written of *The Lord of the Rings*. It helps explain that strange power that compels Tolkien fans to read it over and over again, despite its great length and its massive accumulation of detail. Whether it is our first or our ninth reading, we press on with endurance, for we yearn to reach that eucatastrophe, that sudden and unexpected turn when unlooked-for victory is born out of certain defeat, utter joy out of utter despair. Whether or not we believe in divine providence, the ending nevertheless strikes us with the force of grace, of good news: for the happy ending is both natural and miraculous, the fruit of great struggle and yet totally unmerited.

It is odd that Tolkien, the devout Roman Catholic, would say that there is no word to describe this sudden turn, this "good-catastrophe." There *is* a word, a phrase really, that stands at the very crux of Catholic theology, one which reminds us that the Bible itself fits Tolkien's fairy-tale pattern for the Consolation of the Happy Ending. The phrase is *felix culpa* (Latin for "blessed guilt" or "happy fall"), a phrase that embodies a great and wonderful paradox. The "culpa" refers to the fall of man (Genesis 3), surely the most terrible event in the history of the world. And yet, theologians insist that this tragic event is somehow a *felix* one. What is the solution to this two-word prophetic riddle? The answer is that very evangelium that Tolkien alludes to above. Though the fall was a great evil, God used that evil as a vehicle for pouring out a greater love and blessing upon mankind. The fall is *felix*, that is, because it made possible and necessary the incarnation of Christ. When all seemed lost, when the human race seemed doomed to perpetual misery and death, history took a sudden and unexpected turn. God came down and restored what was broken. The Bible, which starts with a death but ends with a marriage, is not a Tragedy but a Comedy—a true fairy tale replete with Eucatastrophe. It should therefore come as no surprise that the two greatest works of the Christian imagination—*The Divine Comedy* and *The Brothers*

Karamazov—both "indulge" us with Happy Endings, and that the third (*Paradise Lost*) takes as one of its central themes the very *felix culpa* discussed above.

And in case you are wondering: yes, I consider *The Lord of the Rings*—if not fourth in line, then surely in the top ten—to be another of the crowning achievements of the Christian imagination: a tale of fall and redemption, sin and grace, great evil and greater good that provides us with one of the richest eucatastrophic turns in literature.

SAM'S HOPEFUL VISION

Aside from the eucatastrophe, hope is a bauble, a gewgaw, a vain and empty soap bubble. And to many in the modern world, who have lost their faith in the Happy Ending, hope is exactly that. But it is not so for Samwise Gamgee, who knows the old stories and believes in them too (I.ii.62). He has studied and sung the old lays of the elder days, many of which (like that of Beren and Luthien) celebrate the victory that rises up out of the jaws of death. After Sam and Frodo leave Faramir and head for Mordor, it is Sam's hope, more than anything else, that gives Frodo the strength and will to continue on.

When Frodo is held captive in the tower of Cirith Ungol, it is Sam who discovers where he is being held and rescues him: a discovery that is made through the medium of song. Though the darkness and evil of the tower are heavy and oppressive, Sam manages to lift up a song of hope and joy that penetrates the darkness and calls out to Frodo: "Though here at journey's end I lie / in darkness buried deep, / beyond all towers strong and high, / beyond all mountains steep, / above all shadows rides the Sun / and Stars for ever dwell: / I will not say the Day is done, / nor bid the Stars farewell" (VI.i.888). Here, in the second stanza of his song, Sam throws a challenge into the very face of despair. He will give up on neither the sun nor the stars; his hope will remain though he stands on the very brink of doom.

And the stars respond in kind! As the two Hobbits make their way through the filth and desolation of Mordor, Sam is vouch-safed a vision (almost a visitation) that strengthens his hope when it has almost run out:

> There, peeping among the cloud-wrack above a dark tor high up in the mountains, Sam saw a white star twinkle for a while. The beauty of it smote his heart, and he looked up out of the forsaken land, and hope returned to him. For like a shaft, clear and cold, the thought pierced him that in the end the Shadow was only a small and passing thing: there was a light and high beauty for ever beyond its reach. His song in the Tower had been defiance rather than hope; for then he was thinking of himself. Now, for a moment, his own fate, and even his master's, ceased to trouble him. He crawled back into the brambles and laid himself by Frodo's side, and putting away all fear he cast himself into a deep untroubled sleep. (VI.ii.901)

In addition to strengthening his hope, the vision of the white star purifies and reorients it. When he sang his song of defiance in the tower of Cirith Ungol, Sam's focus was only on himself and his master. But now, as the white star draws his vision higher, beyond Mordor and his own personal struggle for survival, Sam perceives the true essence of the theological virtue of hope. Hope is more than an engine for endurance; it is the deep, heartfelt understanding that though we may fail in our mission, and though we may perish alone in the dark, the Shadow *will* pass away and goodness *will* triumph. It does not rest finally on our efforts or struggles. For the Shadow, despite its momentary triumph, can never touch that light and beauty which ever transcends it.

I don't know about you, but when I read this passage I feel exactly that "catch of the breath," that "beat and lifting of the heart" that Tolkien describes so powerfully in "On Fairy-Stories." Even though the actual eucatastrophe does not come until the next chapter, the turn begins here with Sam's hopeful vision—which is also a vision of hope. In its wake, Sam is able to put away his fear and, for the first time in weeks, enjoy a "deep untroubled sleep."

EUCATASTROPHE IN NARNIA

In *The Lion, the Witch and the Wardrobe,* Lewis constructs his own eucatastrophe, one that more closely parallels the *felix culpa* of Christian theology. This time the *culpa* is not initiated by a man and a woman eating a forbidden fruit in a garden (though Lewis would later incorporate that image into *The Magician's Nephew*), but by a spiteful, peevish boy named Edmund eating magical candy in a snowy wood. Rather than being offered to him by a serpent, the candy—which appears at first to be nothing more than an innocent box of Turkish delight—is given to him by a White Witch in a sleigh. In no time at all, the greedy boy devours the entire box of candy and asks the Witch for more, but she tells him that she will only give him more if he comes to her castle and brings with him his brother and two sisters. Alas, Edmund does not realize that what he had just eaten "was enchanted Turkish Delight and that anyone who had once tasted it would want more and more of it, and would even, if they were allowed, go on eating it till they killed themselves" (IV.33). The Turkish delight magnifies Edmund's already strong propensity toward envy and selfishness, and, in the end, he betrays his own siblings to the White Witch. By cleverly conflating the eating of the Turkish delight with Edmund's betrayal, Lewis is able to embody within a single character the sins of both Adam and Judas. And by so doing, he is able to conflate as well the double eucatastrophe latent in the gospel story: the sin of Adam leads to the fall (evil), which leads to the incarnation (good); the sin of Judas leads to the crucifixion (evil), which leads to the resurrection (good).

Once Peter, Susan, and Lucy discover what Edmund has done, they make their way as fast as they can to their destined meeting with Aslan. Aslan greets the three children warmly and then asks where the fourth is. After he has been told that Edmund has betrayed them, Lucy breaks in and asks Aslan if there is not something he can do to save Edmund.

> "All shall be done," said Aslan, "But it may be harder than you think." And then he was silent again for some time. Up to that moment Lucy had been thinking how royal and strong and peaceful his face looked; now it suddenly came into her head that he looked sad as well. (XII.124)

The harder path to which he alludes involves Aslan being sacrificed (like Christ) by the White Witch in the place of Edmund the traitor: a tragic event that will give way—through "a sudden and miraculous grace: never to be counted on to recur"—to his glorious resurrection when dawn breaks on the following morning. Like the Bible, like *The Lord of the Rings*, *The Lion, the Witch and the Wardrobe* has a Happy Ending, but it is one that is suffered and fought for. Neither Aslan nor Lewis is an "escapist," if by that word we mean one who flees from the harsh realities of the world. Sorrow and pain are not to be naïvely dismissed through false optimism, but fully embraced and endured. What is not to be embraced is that despair that would have us believe that all is lost and that evil will triumph forever. The way of the eucatastrophe, as Aslan tries to explain to the despairing Lucy, is very often the harder way, but it is the only way that offers final and lasting hope.

For believers like Tolkien and Lewis, all the eucatastrophes that fill the pages of myth, legend, and fairy tale point either forward or backward to the gospel story. That does not mean however that Christian writers are to therefore cease creating new stories; it means instead that all stories that include the Consolation of the Happy Ending are enriched and ennobled by the myth that became fact. As Tolkien explains in the last paragraph of "On Fairy-Stories":

> The Evangelium has not abrogated legends; it has hallowed them, especially the "happy ending." The Christian has still to work, with mind as well as body, to suffer, hope, and die; but he may now perceive that all his bents and faculties have a purpose, which can be redeemed.

And that is good news indeed!

the LOVE that PITIES and FORGIVES

According to 1 Corinthians 13:13, the greatest of the three theological virtues is love—or, in the King James, charity. It is, I think, a pity that the word *charity* has become reduced in most people's minds to mean only the giving of alms to the poor. The word actually comes from the Latin "caritas," which is itself a translation of the Greek *agape*: both point to a higher kind of love, a more spiritual, self-sacrificing love that gives of itself. Charity, in its older sense, has all the qualities that St. Paul ascribes to it in his great "love chapter"—it is patient, kind, does not envy or boast, does not seek evil for others nor keep a record of wrongs, rejoices in goodness and not in iniquity. It is the supreme virtue that incorporates all the other virtues, just as the greatest commandments (to love the Lord and our neighbor) sum up the Mosaic law. Charity (love) is that which "beareth all things, believeth all things, hopeth all things, endureth all things" (13:7). It is the most active of the three virtues, for while faith and hope can transform the one who possesses them, love can transform not only us but the world around us. In a sense, the difference between faith/hope and love is like the difference between the first Adam and the second (Christ): "The first man Adam was made a living soul; the last Adam was made a quickening [life-giving] spirit" (1 Corinthians 15:45). It is true that faith and hope can often prove "contagious," but love excels them, and all other virtues, in its ability not only to hold life in itself but to give it as well.

Of all the definitions I've read or heard of that most elusive of words, the one that comes closest to capturing love's essence is simply this: love is the movement out of narcissism. The true foe of love is not hate but egocentrism, for hate can often be rechanneled back into love, but egocentrism prevents us from ever moving out of ourselves toward the other. Love is extinguished more quickly by apathy and indifference than it is by either jealousy or wrath. To be healthy, love must be like the River Jordan, a living, flowing conduit linking one sea to the next. When it ceases to flow outward, when it narcissistically holds within itself that which flows into it, then it becomes as stagnant and barren as the Dead Sea.

PITY FOR GOLLUM

When Gandalf tells Frodo about the Ring and how Bilbo took it from its former owner, the hateful Gollum, Frodo responds that it is a pity Bilbo did not kill him. Gandalf replies:

> Pity? It was Pity that stayed his hand. Pity, and Mercy: not to strike without need. And he has been well rewarded, Frodo. Be sure that he took so little hurt from the evil, and escaped in the end, because he began his ownership of the Ring so. With Pity. (I.ii.58)

In chapter V of *The Hobbit*, Tolkien explains the exact nature of Bilbo's pity and how and why it prevented him from killing Gollum when he had the chance.

Through a providential accident, Bilbo, while traveling through the Misty Mountains, tumbles down into the deep, dark lair of Gollum, where he finds, by a second providential accident, the Ring lying on the floor of the cave. Bilbo puts the Ring in his pocket and says nothing about it. Bilbo and Gollum then engage in a game of riddles, with the understanding that if Bilbo loses, Gollum will eat him, but if Gollum loses, he must show Bilbo the way out. Bilbo wins the game (when Gollum cannot guess what he has in his pocket), but Gollum does not keep his end of the bargain. Instead, he paddles off in his boat to get his Ring (which has the power to make its wearer invisible), with the clear intention of using it to enable him to kill with impunity the armed Hobbit. But the foul creature realizes that his Ring is gone, upon which he falls into a rage and rushes after Bilbo. Bilbo meanwhile discovers the magical properties of the Ring and wears it. After a long chase in the dark, Bilbo finds the tunnel that will take him back to the surface, only to discover that Gollum has positioned himself in the center of the passage. Immediately, a hundred conflicting thoughts and emotions rush through Bilbo's mind:

> Bilbo almost stopped breathing, and went stiff himself. He was desperate. He must get away, out of the horrible darkness, while he had any strength left. He must fight. He must stab the foul thing, put its eyes out, kill it. It meant to kill him. No, not a fair fight. He was invisible now. Gollum had no sword. Gollum had not actually threatened to kill him, or tried to yet. And he was miserable, alone, lost. A sudden understanding, a pity mixed with horror, welled up in Bilbo's heart: a glimpse of endless

unmarked days without light or hope of betterment, hard stone, cold fish, sneaking and whispering. All these thoughts passed in a flash of a second. He trembled. And then quite suddenly in another flash, as if lifted up by a new strength and resolve, he leaped.

Bilbo's decision here in the dark of Gollum's cave is one of the pivotal moments—if not *the* pivotal moment—in the long history of the Ring. Had Bilbo begun his possession of the Ring by killing Gollum (as Gollum had begun his possession by murdering his friend Déagol), the Ring would surely have corrupted him as it had Gollum (Gandalf says as much to Frodo). It is only because he shows pity to the miserable creature that Bilbo is left relatively unscathed.

Now, it must be admitted that pity is not always an expression of love. Quite often—as C. S. Lewis demonstrates in *The Screwtape Letters* and *The Great Divorce*—pity can be used to bind, pervert, and manipulate the one on whom it is lavished. But not in Bilbo's case. The pity that stays Bilbo's hand is a pure expression of *caritas* that is born out of Bilbo's ability to move out of himself (out of his fear, hatred, and disgust) and feel a sympathetic (even empathetic) connection with the loathsome and deceptive Gollum. And be assured on this point, Gollum *is* loathsome, both here and throughout *The Lord of the Rings*; he does not, in any human sense, deserve pity, love, or mercy. But then the pity that wells up within Bilbo at this decisive moment is not human but divine. In a flash of what can only be described as divine insight, Bilbo is enabled to see Gollum's misery through Gollum's eyes, to experience vicariously, and therefore understand, the horror of his dark, hopeless condition. It is that insight that allows him to love Gollum as a suffering thing in need of grace. Christ instructs His followers to forgive their enemies, not because they deserve forgiveness, but because He has forgiven us, and we are expected, like the River Jordan, to allow that forgiveness to flow through us to others. Just so, Bilbo takes pity on Gollum, not because he deserves pity but because Bilbo allows himself to be a conduit of a higher pity.

It is this lesson that Gandalf tries to convey to Frodo when he tells him that pity stayed the hand of Bilbo, but Frodo remains confused. He does not understand why Gandalf, who had earlier captured Gollum, did not take the opportunity to kill him for his crimes. Surely, Frodo exclaims, Gollum deserves death. To which Gandalf responds,

> Deserves it! I daresay he does. Many that live deserve death. And some that die deserve life. Can you give it to them? Then do not be too eager to deal out death in judgement. For even the very wise cannot see all ends. I have not much hope that Gollum can be cured before he dies, but there is a chance of it. And he is bound up with the fate of the Ring. My heart tells me he has some part to play yet, for good or ill, before the end; and when that comes, the pity of Bilbo may rule the fate of many—yours not least. (I.ii.58)

Love, pity, and forgiveness, Gandalf here suggests, not only rest on our ability to move out of ourselves and see the misery of the other, but on our humble acceptance of the fact that we do not have perfect vision: that we do not see all ends. There are many forces at work, both in Tolkien's world and our own, and no one can fathom them all, not even the wise Gandalf.

Book IV of *The Lord of the Rings*, during which Gollum becomes, through yet another strange twist of fate, the guide for Frodo and Sam, might best be subtitled "The education of Frodo." For it is during these chapters that Frodo slowly learns to feel pity and even love for Gollum. And it is a pity that is based primarily on his ability to sympathize with Gollum's fate, to realize, in all humility, how easily he might, like Gollum, become corrupted by the Ring. Much to the consternation and confusion of Sam, he even begins to treat Gollum kindly, calling him by his real name (Sméagol), the name he bore before the Ring perverted and reduced him to the pathetic Gollum. But Frodo's kindness is not equivalent to blindness, to use Tolkien's own words; his is a "bold love" that is fully aware of the untrustworthy nature of Gollum. He loves but also keeps his guard; toward Gollum, he is, to quote Christ's own counsel, both innocent as a dove and wise as a serpent (Matthew 10:16). And, miraculously, Gollum responds to his gentle but firm love, so much so that, for a time, Sméagol peeps through.

In the end, tragically, Gollum returns to his evil path, but the love previously shown him by Bilbo, Gandalf, and Frodo transforms the evil intentions of Gollum into a good end. Had any of the three good characters followed their angry impulses and killed Gollum, the evil creature would not have been present at the end of the journey to save the life (and soul) of Frodo . . . and that of Middle-earth as well. For it is, miraculously, Gollum who effects the eucatastrophe that turns defeat (as he stands at the edge of Mount Doom, Frodo chooses not to cast in the Ring but to keep it for himself) into victory (Gollum bites the Ring from Frodo's finger and then falls, Ring in hand, into the Cracks of Doom). Love has molded Gollum (the most unlikely of vessels) into a conduit for grace, and, though he is not a willing vessel, he proves an effective one.

Frodo's pity paves the way for this miraculous turn of events, but his pity alone is not enough. Shortly before Gollum takes back the Ring from Frodo, Sam is given the chance to do what he has long wanted: to kill Gollum. However, when Gollum begs for mercy, something speaks deep within Sam's heart, the same voice that spoke to Bilbo so many years before:

> Sam's hand wavered. His mind was hot with wrath and the memory of evil. It would be just to slay this treacherous, murderous creature, just and many times deserved; and also it seemed the only safe thing to do. But deep in his heart there was something that restrained him: he could not strike this thing lying in the dust, forlorn, ruinous, utterly wretched. He himself, though only for a little while, had borne the Ring, and now dimly he guessed the agony of Gollum's shrivelled mind and body, enslaved to that Ring, unable to find peace or relief ever in life again. But Sam had no words to express what he felt. (VI. iii.923)

Sam reasons truthfully when he thinks it would be both just and practical to kill Gollum, yet still he stays his hand. Sam's pity, like that of Frodo, is prompted in great part by his ability to empathize with the misery of Gollum, but it is also prompted, surely, by Frodo's example. That is to say, *both* Gollum and Sam are transformed by Frodo's love, though only Sam accepts the transformation and allows it to redefine him. Sam has done more than choose to act (or not act) in a certain way; he has chosen as well to be a different kind of person.

As Mordor falls to ruins around them (in response to the destruction of the Ring), Frodo turns to Sam and tells him that Gollum has played his role in the Quest, and that they must both now forgive him. The usually talkative Sam says nothing in reply; his silence gives assent.

ASLAN'S TRANSFORMING LOVE

Throughout the Chronicles of Narnia, the love and forgiveness of Aslan transforms the lives of all those who come in contact with him. His boundless *caritas* and mercy are the bridge over which Edmund crosses from spiteful traitor to valiant warrior (*The Lion, the Witch and the Wardrobe*); Trumpkin develops from stubborn skeptic to loyal follower (*Prince Caspian*); Eustace expands from small-minded pest to broad-minded explorer (*The Voyage of the Dawn Treader*); Jill matures from vain, self-centered girl to humble, heroic young lady (*The Silver Chair*); Shasta rises from provincial rustic to courteous knight (*The Horse and His Boy*); and Tirian evolves from rash, headstrong youth to fearless martyr (*The Last Battle*).

And then there is Digory, who begins *The Magician's Nephew* by performing an act of bravery (when he goes in pursuit of a girl named Polly whom his wicked uncle Andrew has sent into another world via a magic ring) but then compromises this noble act by giving in (like Eve) to the lust for forbidden knowledge. On account of his sin, Digory awakens the evil Queen Jadis, and, through a series of events, brings her into the newly created world of Narnia. Aslan, who sings Narnia into being, knows what has happened and that Digory is to blame for it, but instead of scolding or accusing him, he asks him if he is ready to undo the wrong he has done. Digory is ready, but he also has something else on his mind. Back in our world, Digory's mother is dying, and the boy wonders if Aslan, who has just created an entire world, can't do something to restore his mother's health. Though fear is heavy upon him, he blurts out his need to Aslan:

> "But please, please — won't you — can't you give me something
> that will cure Mother." Up till then he had been looking at the

Lion's great front feet and the huge claws on them; now, in his despair, he looked up at its face. What he saw surprised him as much as anything in his whole life. For the tawny face was bent down near his own and (wonder of wonders) great shining tears stood in the Lion's eyes. They were such big, bright tears compared with Digory's own that for a moment he felt as if the Lion must really be sorrier about his Mother than he was himself. (XII.142)

Just as Jesus weeps before the tomb of Lazarus (and thus shows not only His own personal grief but His solidarity with the grief of humanity), so Aslan sheds tears for the sorrow of Digory and the pain of his mother. The Lion loves and pities both mother and son with a compassion that is even greater than Digory's own. The sight of those tears transforms Digory, for he now knows that even if Aslan does not heal his mother, he understands fully, and shares fully in, his grief.

In the chapters that follow, Digory is commissioned to pluck and bring back to Aslan a magic apple from a tree in a walled, Edenic garden. He does so, but then is accosted by Jadis, who tempts him to steal the apple and bring it back home to heal his mother. This time, however, Digory (unlike Eve) resists the temptation of forbidden knowledge; he stays loyal to Aslan. But the choice is not an easy one. "He was very sad," Lewis tells us, "and he wasn't even sure all the time that he had done the right thing: but whenever he remembered the shining tears in Aslan's eyes he became sure" (XIII.164).

Held firm in the love of Aslan, Digory can bear, believe, hope, and endure all things.

PART FOUR

Evil

CHAPTER THIRTEEN

FORBIDDEN FRUIT

The story is told a hundred different ways in a hundred different cultures. The young, untested hero travels blissfully along the road in search of adventure and meets, instead, the devil. And there, at the crossroads, he sells his soul for a "year at the top." It matters little what his dearly bought year will bring him — fame, fortune, romance, talent. It matters even less if his initial motivation seems honorable: to unlock the secrets of immortality (like Dr. Frankenstein) or to release mankind from his bestial side (like Dr. Jekyll) or to bring about world peace (like Captain Nemo). Indeed, he may not even meet the devil. What he encounters at the crossroads may simply be the lure of forbidden knowledge . . . and of the power that such knowledge always promises to bring.

These Faustian heroes (antiheroes?) have always been with us, but their numbers vastly increased, and have continued to increase, since the French Revolution inspired (infected?) the Western world with a belief that man's potential is unlimited and that he is the maker of his own destiny. In the wake of the revolution, the British poet Lord Byron wrote a dozen or so popular verse romances about young heroes who commit an unforgivable sin and, as a result, become lonely wanderers and outcasts who can no longer dwell within the circle of humanity. Though these "oriental tales" have been all but forgotten today, their moody, passionate, tormented protagonists captured the imagination of Europe and ensured that such figures would henceforth bear the generic title of Byronic Hero.

The life cycle of the Byronic Hero always begins with the breaching of some type of taboo (Adam eating the forbidden fruit; Cain killing his brother; Prometheus stealing the fire; Oedipus marrying his mother; the Ancient Mariner shooting the albatross): an act that, whether nobly or basely motivated, manifests itself ultimately as an act of rebellion and defiance. They soon discover that the fruit is sour, that their action has made them both a curse and a contagion, but they have progressed too far in their sin to go back and, in any case, are too proud to seek forgiveness (Macbeth, Heathcliff, Ahab, Dorian Gray). For Christians, the ultimate example of this figure is Satan, the fallen archangel who is not only himself the great Byronic Hero but who would—in accordance with the ethos of hell: misery loves company—tempt all of us to become little Byronic Heroes. For those who reject the literal existence of the Devil, the Byronic Hero reaches its fullest embodiment in Satan's legendary, mythopoeic counterpart: Count Dracula, the Prince of Darkness, who lives on the borders of society, feeds on human blood, and fears the cross. Indeed, popular culture in America is overrun with Byronic Heroes: from the Mummy and the Wolfman to the Highlander and Darth Vader to the innumerable dark, vigilante-like superheroes who populate the pages of comic books and graphic novels and who have come to dominate movie screens since the late 1990s. It is not too much to say that our modern (and now postmodern) age is obsessed with the Byronic Hero, with his willingness to risk all for forbidden knowledge, his self-inflicted torment and agony, his tragic greatness.

While Tolkien and Lewis understood well the lure of the Byronic Hero, they also saw the dangers in holding up such a figure for emulation. They saw, in short, that beneath the angst, the rage, and the over-self-consciousness of the Byronic Hero lay not the triumph of man but his destruction, not the romance of Nietzsche's Superman but the sin of Father Adam.

GOLLUM AS BYRONIC HERO

In the previous two sections, we considered closely how Tolkien and Lewis embodied the classical and theological virtues in the lives, actions, and choices of their heroes. I would like to shift the focus now away from those virtues to consider how *The Lord of the Rings* and The Chronicles of Narnia also explore the nature of evil in the lives, actions, and choices of their villains. That is not to say that either Tolkien or Lewis saw their heroes as all virtuous and their villains as all vicious. To the contrary, Tolkien and Lewis, as orthodox Christians, understood that all have sinned and fallen short of the glory of God, that we are all volatile mixtures of good and evil, that our nature lies midway between the angel above and the beast below. Indeed, I have chosen to focus this chapter on the Byronic Hero, for he, as someone whose fall is motivated as much by his noble as his base qualities, offers the perfect transition from the virtues that inspire and uplift us to the sins that degrade and devour our God-given glory and potential.

It is no exaggeration to say that the entire *Lord of the Rings*, and the greater narrative of the War of the Ring of which it is a part, would not have occurred had it not been for a single, tragic choice made by a Byronic Hero. I speak, of course, of Isildur, the mighty forefather of Aragorn who cut the Ring from Sauron's finger at the end of the Second Age, but then refused the advice of Elrond to cast it into the fires of Mount Doom. Had he done so, Sauron would have been destroyed, but Isildur's lust of the eye, lust of the flesh, and pride of life (see 1 John 2:16) drove him to keep for himself the forbidden fruit of the One Ring. Before Isildur, in the far-off days of the First Age, Tolkien placed an even grander and more overpowering Byronic Hero, the Noldor Elf Fëanor, the maker of the Silmarils (sacred, magical jewels; see *The Silmaril-lion*), and after him, in *The Lord of the Rings*, Tolkien placed a third, the noble but headstrong Boromir. All three heroes are larger-than-life warriors of prodigious skill and courage, unafraid to face evil and to risk certain death for a worthy cause; but all three sur-render in the end to the lure of forbidden fruit. Just as their lust for the precious silver, mithril, caused the Dwarfs of Moria to dig too deep and awaken the Balrog, so Fëanor's lust for the beauty and power of the Silmarils, and Isildur and Boromir's for that of the Ring, led them down the path of destruction.

Still, if we are to delve into Tolkien's vital critique of the dan-gers of the Byronic Hero, then we must look past these three warriors—all of whom die soon enough after their fatal choice to retain and even regain much of their dignity—and focus on a more humble figure (Gollum) in whom we see the sin of Adam magnified and drawn out over a lifetime of misery and corruption.

With the warriors, we find Tolkien working more in the Greco-Roman epic tradition (with Fëanor embodying the tragic wrath of Achilles, Isildur the tragic pride of Julius Caesar, and Boromir the tragic misjudgment of Brutus); with Gollum, he moves on to Judeo-Christian ground to offer an incisive portrait of a soul twisted and broken by obsession and greed (one that can be profitably compared with that of the splenetic, misanthropic narrator of Dostoevsky's *Notes from Underground*). Dante writes in Canto III of *Inferno* that the damned souls actually yearn for the very thing they most fear and dread; in the same way, Gollum's unlawful desire to possess the Ring (his "precious") is the very thing that causes him pain and despair. The Ring whispers in his ear that it will make him great and wise and powerful, but it does not deliver on its promises. Rather, like the thief of John 10:10, it steals his humanity, kills his joy, and destroys his peace. It leaves him an empty shell, repulsive to man and beast alike.

And, let this be clear, Gollum *is* a wholly repulsive creature. The mercy that Bilbo, Gandalf, and Frodo extend toward him (see previous chapter) is truly Christ-like; it is not motivated by anything "loveable" in Gollum. With remarkable psychological, emotional, and spiritual precision, Tolkien presents Gollum to us as a Byronic Hero who has been stripped of all his romantic allure and fashionable angst. Like Ahab, he is megalomaniacally focused on a single objective, but he does not command the fear or awe of a crew of sailors; like Heathcliff, he wanders lonely and companionless through a world of desolation, but he lacks a passionate love to humanize him; like the Fisher King, he is as desolate within as the world around him, but his wound will not be healed; like Oedipus and Prometheus, he suffers terrible torments, but his sufferings neither heal a city nor provide the light of knowledge to mankind. In Gollum, all the pretensions of the Byronic Hero are exploded, revealed for what they are at the core: vanity, disobedience, avarice. In a word, sin.

The "inmates" of Dante's Inferno try their best to preserve their dignity and to present themselves as nobly tragic, but they can no longer fool anyone. The nature of their sin is written plainly for all to see in the nature of their punishment. Neither can Gollum fool anyone as to his inner state of depravity. He may rejoice that the Ring has extended his life indefinitely, but it is not a life to be envied. Consider the West's ongoing fascination with zombies, vampires, werewolves, and mummies. Do not all these creatures, like the Frankenstein monster itself, represent varying incarnations of the walking dead? All, in their own way, possess a form of immortality that is really a living death. Just so, Gollum's "life" is wholly lacking in love, in peace, in purpose. He simply goes on, like a gnawing toothache or a perpetual grudge. Death for him would be a release, a mercy, yet he must continue on, yearning joylessly and hopelessly to regain the very thing that robbed him of his joy and hope. The problem with sin, with evil, is not that it is fun, but that it dehumanizes us, choking with soot and ash that initial divine spark that God breathed into the nostrils of history's first Byronic Hero.

I said above that the fullest legendary embodiment of the Byronic Hero is Count Dracula, and Gollum, in his lonely nighttime existence (he hates not only the sun but the moon as well) and his penchant for raw food, is very much a vampire-like creature. But the similarity goes deeper than that. Just as Dracula cannot abide the sight of a cross, the presence of the Host, or the touch of holy water, so Gollum is actually hurt by the good magic of the elves. When Frodo ties one end of an elvish rope to Gollum's ankle, the miserable creature, Tolkien tells us, "began to scream, a thin, tearing sound, very horrible to hear. He writhed, and tried to get his mouth to his ankle and bite the rope. He kept on screaming" (IV.i.603). The mere touch of the rope hurts Gollum as deeply as the Nazgûl blade that pierces Frodo on Weathertop. A similar reaction occurs when Frodo and Sam graciously offer Gollum some of their elvish waybread (lembas); rather than quench his hunger and restore his strength, as it does for the Hobbits, the waybread chokes Gollum as though he had ingested "dust and ashes" (IV.i.608). As Tolkien clearly meant the lembas to represent the communion wafer, the link between Gollum's hatred of the lembas and Dracula's hatred of the Host is particularly strong. Yet again, as the three pass through the ruined gardens of Gondor, the Hobbits and Gollum have a startlingly different reaction to a thing whose beauty and virtue borders on the sacramental: "As they walked, brushing their way through bush and herb, sweet odours rose about them. Gollum coughed and retched; but the Hobbits breathed deep, and suddenly Sam laughed, for heart's ease not for jest" (IV.iv.636). Like Dracula, Gollum's reactions to that which is good and holy have been thrown out of whack. He not only yearns for what he fears, but rejects as poison the very things that might cure him.

Shakespeare begins *Macbeth* by having his witches declare that fair is foul and foul is fair, a twisted ethos Macbeth will embrace after he commits his taboo sin. Just so, Gollum's embrace of the Ring strands him in a topsy-turvy world where life is death and death is life.

"A High and Lonely Destiny"

If Tolkien's depiction of Gollum gives the lie to the romantic exaltation of the Faustian hero who lusts for forbidden knowledge and power, then Lewis's depiction of Uncle Andrew and Queen Jadis (in *The Magician's Nephew*) gives the lie to the equally romantic exaltation of the satanic hero who rebels against all authority and who would prefer to rule in hell than to serve in heaven. As a Milton scholar (and author of *A Preface to Paradise Lost*), Lewis was well aware that the same revolutionary spirit that celebrated the Byronic Hero had declared Satan, and not God, to be the true hero of Milton's epic. This grave misunderstanding of Milton, and of the Bible, troubled Lewis greatly, not only in its original Romantic form but in the more virulent form it took in the writings of Nietzsche, who argued that the true hero is one whose taboo-shattering charisma allows him to rise above all bourgeois morality ("beyond good and evil") to assert his own satanic will to power. Like Tolkien, Lewis uses the villains of his "fairy tale" to expose the true antilife spirit that lurks beneath the noble façade of the Byronic Hero.

Both Andrew and Jadis are fully convinced that they possess a "high and lonely destiny" that permits (nay, commands) them to break whatever rules they must to achieve their lofty aims. In the case of Andrew, he is quite willing to sacrifice the lives of children to further his occult studies. When he is confronted by his nephew Digory on this point and accused of having acted in a "rotten" fashion, Andrew reacts with puzzlement:

> Rotten? . . . Oh, I see. You mean that little boys ought to keep their promises. Very true: most right and proper, I'm sure, and I'm very glad you have been taught to do it. But of course you must understand that rules of that sort, however excellent they may be for little boys — and servants — and women — and even people in general, can't possibly be expected to apply to profound students and great thinkers and sages. No, Digory. Men

like me who possess hidden wisdom, are freed from common rules just as we are cut off from common pleasures. Ours, my boy, is a high and lonely destiny. (II.18)

With one fell stroke, Lewis rips wide open a century of empty rhetoric that would justify sin and evil by appealing to some vague mandate that transcends the boundaries of biblical ethics. The pretensions of every "mad scientist" from Dr. Frankenstein to Dr. Jekyll, every murderer from Cain to Raskolnikov, and every revolutionary tyrant from Napoleon to Mao are laid bare in such a way that even a child can see through them.

Then Lewis does it again several chapters later, when he has Jadis justify her destruction of all her people by speaking the Deplorable Word: for which forbidden knowledge she paid a high price. When Digory confronts *her*, she is equally puzzled by his "schoolboy ethics":

> I had forgotten that you are only a common boy. How should you understand reasons of State? You must learn, child, that what would be wrong for you or for any of the common people is not wrong in a great Queen such as I. The weight of the world is on our shoulders. We must be freed from all rules. Ours is a high and lonely destiny. (V.62)

Digory recognizes at once that Jadis has used the same words as Uncle Andrew, but, Lewis perceptively notes, they sound grander coming from her "because Uncle Andrew was not seven feet tall and dazzlingly beautiful." Fairy tales are often accused of prettifying hard truths. In the hands of masters like Lewis and Tolkien, they are more likely to strip away prettified lies.

CHAPTER FOURTEEN

PERVERSION *and* CORRUPTION

The attentive reader of Dante's *Inferno* will quickly notice that everything in hell is a perversion or corruption of something in heaven or on earth. Thus, hell boasts landscapes and venues that resemble those one might find on earth (forests, rivers, deserts, cemeteries, latrines) but in a grotesque, twisted form. Whereas in heaven, the circle represents eternity and perfection, in hell it represents unending futility. Many of the beasts who staff hell (the Minotaur, the Centaurs, Geryon) possess a dual nature that mocks that of Christ, while the chief "beast" (Satan himself) boasts three heads—a perversion, of course, of the triune nature of the Christian God. As for the punishments, that for simony (buying and selling church offices) is a parody of the sacrament of baptism, that for evil counsel is a parody of the flaming tongues of Pentecost, and that for heresy is a parody of the resurrection of the body.

In so constructing hell, Dante sought not only to impress his readers with his ingenuity, but to embody poetically a central truth of Christian theology: namely, that evil is not a positive or creative entity but a privation, a negation of that which is good, true, and beautiful. In the writings of the fathers of the church, especially Augustine, evil is never portrayed as an equal and opposing power set over against goodness. Evil is neither created nor self-sustaining. It is, rather, a parasite on goodness. Just as a tear in a shirt owes its "existence" to the shirt and would cease to have any existence if it were removed from the shirt, so evil does not possess within itself a life-force separate from that of God. To paraphrase a line from Lewis's *Mere Christianity*, God's eternal, uncreated life is the only energy on which the universe runs. Were God to remove that energy from Satan, Satan would immediately cease to exist. Satan is not the yin to God's yang; he is a creature (like us) who rebelled: an angel who went bad.

Of course, to deny to Satan a separate existence is not to reduce him to a mere psychological phenomenon. Satan is a real being, just as the archangels Michael and Gabriel are real beings, though none of them possesses a physical body as we humans do. Still, the complete dependency of Satan on God, of evil on goodness, cannot be stressed enough. When I speak of evil (as I did in the previous chapter) as being anti-joy and anti-peace, I do not mean to imply that evil offers a competing form of joy and peace. What evil does is take these fruits of the Spirit and corrupt them: as disease corrupts health or pollution corrupts the air and water. To paraphrase *Mere Christianity* again, whereas goodness shall one day reach perfection, evil can never succeed in being pure evil.

Evil creates nothing; it only destroys or perverts what goodness has already made.

THE END OF CORRUPTION

Again and again throughout *The Lord of the Rings*, Tolkien makes it abundantly clear that all of his villains—from Sauron to Saruman to Wormtongue to Gollum—were once good. Indeed, Tolkien's Augustinian understanding of evil as negation is summed up succinctly in two sentences spoken by Elrond at the council at Rivendell: "For nothing is evil in the beginning. Even Sauron was not so" (II.ii.261). It is imperative that the members of the Fellowship keep these sage words in mind as they travel on their long, weary road. Only by so doing can they understand the nature of what they are fighting and resist it with courage and hope.

Neither Sauron nor Mordor can remain forever. Goodness, Truth, Beauty: all are primary and all will prevail in the end. They existed before the soul of Sauron and the soil of Mordor grew black and perverse, and they will remain long after Sauron has been destroyed and Mordor restored to its original fecundity. Tolkien's harrowing descriptions of Mordor conjure in the reader's mind an image of a land turned inside out: the world as it might have been had it been constructed by frauds and falsifiers (see the tenth level of the eighth circle of Dante's *Inferno* for a disturbing portrait of what such a world might look like). Treebeard tells Merry and Pippin that "Trolls are only counterfeits, made by the Enemy in the Great Darkness, in mockery of Ents, as Orcs were of Elves" (III.iv.474); in the same way, Mordor, circled round by mountains on every side, is a corruption of our original home: that green Eden that Christian poets like Milton were wont to describe as a walled garden of delight.

But the perversion cannot abide. In the end, all things will return to their original goodness and all names (to paraphrase a line from *The Lion, the Witch and the Wardrobe*) will be returned to their proper owners. Of this great truth, Sam and Frodo catch a glimpse as they prepare to ascend the stairs of Cirith Ungol and make their way into Mordor. In what is to me one of the most luminous (and numinous) moments in the novel, the two Hobbits come upon the broken statue of one of the former kings of Gondor. The head of the statue is gone, "and in its place [is] set in mockery a round rough-hewn stone, rudely painted by savage hands in the likeness of a grinning face with one large red eye in the midst of its forehead" (IV.vii.687). What Sauron has done to Mordor, his evil henchmen have done to the statue of the king: reduced it to a mockery, a perversion of its original self. But even this small-scale perversion cannot endure. As the sun descends in the sky, its beams catch the severed head of the statue (which lies rolled away alongside the road) and restores to it its former crown:

> The eyes were hollow and the carven beard was broken, but about the high stern forehead there was a coronal of silver and gold. A trailing plant with flowers like small white stars had bound itself across the brows as if in reverence for the fallen king, and in the crevices of his stony hair yellow stonecrop gleamed. (IV.vii.687)

As he gazes with wonder upon the natural crown, Frodo exclaims that the enemy cannot conquer forever. The vision—or, better, sign—promises that life will return no matter how cruelly and perversely the enemy might twist it.

Saruman's Destruction

Ironically, if Mordor is a perversion of the Edenic walled garden, then Isengard (the headquarters of Saruman) is a perversion of a perversion. There is still something vaguely natural about Mordor (it reminds me of the Valley of Ashes in *The Great Gatsby* or the water-starved Wasteland of Eliot's epic poem), but Isengard is more steel than soil, more mechanical than natural. Saruman has taken one of the glorious centers of the old kingdom of Gondor and converted it into a munitions factory. Tolkien hated the urban sprawl and industrialization that was polluting the English countryside, and his descriptions of Isengard capture with great pathos the scourge inflicted on England by the unchecked demand for increased production:

> The plain, too, was bored and delved. Shafts were driven deep into the ground; their upper ends were covered by low mounds and domes of stone, so that in the moonlight the Ring of Isengard looked like a graveyard of unquiet dead. For the ground trembled. The shafts ran down by many slopes and spiral stairs to caverns far under; there Saruman had treasuries, store-houses, armouries, smithies, and great furnaces. Iron wheels revolved there endlessly, and hammers thudded. At night plumes of vapour steamed from the vents, lit from beneath with red light, or blue, or venomous green. (III.viii.541)

All that is natural or human has been stripped away by Saruman, who once cared for growing things but who now (Treebeard tells us) has a mind of "metal and wheels" (III.iv.462). Like a mad scientist, Saruman runs roughshod over all the codes and standards he once held sacred. He has truly created a monster.

And, in the middle of his foul-smelling and unnaturally colored monstrosity, he has erected—really reshaped and "improved"—an enormous black tower called Orthanc. Saruman considers it his crowning achievement, a testimony to the brave new world that he will build and rule when the One Ring is his — but, Tolkien informs us, the tower betrays his true status:

> Saruman had slowly shaped [Isengard and Orthanc] to his
> shifting purposes, and made it better, as he thought, being
> deceived — for all those arts and subtle devices, for which he for-
> sook his former wisdom, and which fondly he imagined were his
> own, came but from Mordor; so that what he made was naught,
> only a little copy, a child's model or a slave's flattery, of that
> vast fortress, armoury, prison, furnace of great power, Barad-
> dûr, the Dark Tower, which suffered no rival, and laughed at
> flattery, biding its time, secure in its pride and its immeasurable
> strength. (III.viii.542).

With the insight of a theologian, Tolkien here exposes the finally
servile nature of evil. Saruman thinks he is the master when he
is really the slave, an innovator when he is only an ape. Saruman
cannot be truly creative for to be so he must have wisdom, and
evil is the negation of wisdom. Indeed, he did not even build the
original Tower, only perverted it. Evil, in its pride and folly, rejects
the fear of the Lord, and without that, there can be neither wisdom
nor creativity.

And, though Tolkien does not say it directly in *The Lord of the
Rings*, Sauron's Dark Tower is almost surely a perversion of the
evil fortress of Thangorodrim, built by the "fallen angel" Morgoth
in the First Age (see *The Silmarillion*), even as Thangorodrim is itself a perversion of the beautiful towers and structures built by the
angelic Valar (of whom Morgoth, like Lucifer, was once the most
beautiful: before he fell into corruption). And the layers upon layers of perversion stretch even further. For when Treebeard allows
the defeated Saruman to leave Isengard, he immediately goes to
the Shire and helps convert that most green and edenic of valleys

into a little Isengard, complete with an industrial mill that pollutes the water and air.

And then there is Shelob's Lair, the full horror of which Tolkien conveys in a single sentence: "Out of it came a stench, not the sickly odour of decay in the meads of Morgul, but a foul reek, as if filth unnameable were piled and hoarded in the dark within" (IV. ix.701). If we see in the fortresses of Thangorodrim, Barad-dûr, and Isengard (and in the warped souls of their lords) a specifically masculine type of perversion, then in the lair of Shelob, and in the bloated spider herself, we find a form of corruption that is more distinctly feminine. Shelob represents, at least in part, the maternal, domestic spirit turned inside out: she does not nurture but devours, does not make a home but fouls a den. Tolkien describes her as the very antithesis of feminine beauty: "Great horns she had, and behind her short stalk-like neck was her huge swollen body, a vast bloated bag, swaying and sagging between her legs; its great bulk was black, blotched with livid marks, but the belly underneath was pale and luminous and gave forth a stench" (IV. ix.709). Next to her, even the loathsome Gollum seems attractive.

Shelob marks the ultimate end of that negation that lies at the core of evil. She cares nothing for the kind of power and martial might sought after by Sauron and his ilk, nor does she take any pleasure in her infamy. She desires only "death for all others, mind and body, and for herself a glut of life, alone, swollen till the mountains could no longer hold her up and the darkness could not contain her" (IV.ix.707).

THE PERVERSION OF NARNIA

Like Tolkien, Lewis presents us as well with evil in its masculine and feminine forms. In the characters of King Miraz (*Prince Caspi-*

an) and Prince Rabadash (*The Horse and His Boy*), we meet villains who have perverted their roles as political and military leaders of their people. The former suppresses the talking animals and living trees that it is his duty to protect, while the latter, in an act of cowardice and treachery, carries out a terrorizing raid on Archenland. Miraz reduces Narnia to a police state; Rabadash brings shame upon those very codes of chivalry by which he purports to live his life. In the end, Miraz falls victim to two lords who have obviously drunk deeply of the corruption of his court. Just as Saruman is killed by his broken, dehumanized lackey, Wormtongue, so Miraz is stabbed to death by his own Machiavellian advisors. As for Rabadash, he has himself become so thoroughly dehumanized by his embrace of evil that it seems altogether fitting and natural when Aslan transforms him into a donkey.

The corrupting power of evil takes on a more feminine face in the characters of the White Witch (*The Lion, the Witch and the Wardrobe*) and the Emerald Witch (*The Silver Chair*), both of whom (like Lady Macbeth) twist and pervert their feminine roles and identities. The White Witch acts the part of an anti-mother to the peevish Edmund, enflaming his natural propensity to envy and spite and using it to reduce him to slavish treachery. The Emerald Witch, on the other hand, plays the role of anti-wife to the enchanted Prince Rilian, helping him to become not a just and noble king but a tyrant and dictator. Whereas the good mother and wife seeks to foster self-reliance in her son and self-initiative in her husband, Lewis's two witches stifle and strangle the identities and potentialities of those in their care. Like Shelob, the White Witch is bloated with the lives of those she has devoured (by turning them to stone); like Shelob's Lair, the Kingdom of the Emerald Witch (Underland) is devoid of all light, life, and joy.

However, of all the Chronicles of Narnia, the one that most fully explores the true nature of evil is *The Last Battle*. In this, the final Chronicle, Lewis focuses not on a single villain but on a growing mood of perversion and corruption that poisons Narnia and brings about her destruction. As in the final book of the Bible, *The Last Battle* offers us both an actual antichrist (in the form of Puzzle, a foolish donkey who is manipulated by the avaricious ape Shift into wearing a lion's skin and pretending to be Aslan) and a more general *spirit* of antichrist that infects the hearts, minds, and souls of the Narnians. Deceived by what they think are the commands of the real Aslan, the citizens of Narnia temporarily (in some cases permanently) lose their moral compass and embrace a false and debased version of orthodox Narnian theology: namely, that Tash (the heathen god of the Calormenes) and Aslan are actually the same god (Tashlan). Ethical relativism, *The Last Battle* demonstrates, cannot function as a substitute for theism. Far from providing a viable alternative for structuring society, relativism marks a falling away from and a negation of the theistic truth that we are created beings accountable to a Creator who has fixed His moral code within each of us — even in those who choose to violate it. Indeed, relativism cannot survive apart from the truth it seeks to subvert. In the end, it is destined to implode and deconstruct: as Mordor and Underland do when Sauron is destroyed and the Emerald Witch is first revealed and then slain in her true, perverse serpentine form.

CHAPTER FIFTEEN

BLINDED
by the LIGHT

J ohn begins his gospel on a scale that is as grand and cosmic as the book of Genesis:

> In the beginning was the Word, and the Word was with God, and the Word was God. He was in the beginning with God; all things were made through him, and without him was not anything made that was made. In him was life, and the life was the light of men. The light shines in the darkness, and the darkness has not overcome it. (1:1–5 RSV)

The Word is Christ, the second Person of the Trinity, He who reveals to us the unseen God. In Him dwells in eternal perfection that very light, life, and creative energy of which evil is a privation and negation. More than that, John suggests, these three things that dwell in the Word are inseparable: the power of creativity is the power of life, and the power of life is also the source and origin of light. Apart from that light, there is no life, and apart from the divine spark of creativity, there is neither light nor life.

I argued in the previous chapter that evil entails a perversion and corruption of that life and light that exist only in God. Here, John leads us deeper by asserting that darkness (evil) is *completely* powerless in the face of the divine light (goodness). But the truth lies even deeper than that. Though the Revised Standard Version is correct when it translates verse five as "the darkness has not overcome it," its translation does not (and cannot) capture the full meaning of the original Greek. The word translated "overcome" is *katalambanō*, a word whose root meaning is "to grasp." A man, however, can grasp something in at least two different ways: he can grasp it with his hands (and hence "overcome" it) or grasp it with his mind (and hence "comprehend" it). In the King James Version, the translators opt for the second meaning and translate the phrase "the darkness comprehended it not." Both translations are, of course, correct, though I would argue that "overcome" represents the simple, primary meaning of the verse, while "comprehend" captures the deeper, secondary meaning that lies behind John's assertion. Not only is darkness unable to overcome the light; it cannot even comprehend it. Or, to put it another way, even if it had the power to overcome the light, the darkness could not begin to do so, for it is wholly ignorant of the nature and "mind" of the light it opposes.

"THE DARKNESS HAS NOT OVERCOME IT"

In his version of the Genesis account, *Ainulindale* and *Valaquenta* (anthologized in *The Silmarillion*), Tolkien makes a point similar to John concerning the inability of evil to fathom the light, life, and creativity of the Creator. According to Tolkien, only the Creator (Ilúvatar) has any true knowledge of or access to the Secret Fire by which he fashioned the world and drew it out of the Void. Though he does so with the assistance of the Valar (angelic beings which he created directly before the beginning of time or space), Ilúvatar alone possesses that Fire which is both life and light to the world. Though the Valar consider it a joy and a privilege to share in a work whose origin and purpose is Ilúvatar's, the chief Valar (Melkor, later called Morgoth) sinfully desires to be the sole architect of his own work. Thus, while Ilúvatar leads the Valar in a Song of Creation in which each Valar is allowed a central, if ancillary, role, Melkor sings his own song in defiance of Ilúvatar. Needless to say, Melkor's song is both ugly and perverse and lies at the root of much of the evil recounted in *The Silmarillion*, *The Hobbit*, and *The Lord of the Rings*.

In *Valaquenta*, Tolkien describes the evil and miserable state of Melkor in a way that both parallels the biblical fall of Lucifer and comments powerfully on John 1:5:

> From splendour [Melkor] fell through arrogance to contempt
> for all things save himself, a spirit wasteful and pitiless. Understanding he turned to subtlety in perverting to his own will
> all that he would use until he became a liar without shame. He
> began with the desire of Light, but when he could not possess
> it for himself alone, he descended through fire and wrath into a
> great burning, down into Darkness. And darkness he used most
> in his evil works upon Arda [Earth], and filled it with fear for all
> living things.

The initial desire of Melkor is for the Light — as it is for all creatures fashioned by he who is the Father of Lights — but he is unable to grasp (overcome *or* comprehend) that Light and so he embraces darkness instead. He cannot harness the Secret Fire of Creation, so he becomes lord of that lesser fire that consumes and destroys. It is he who creates the Balrogs (fire demons), one of whom Gandalf resists on the Bridge of Khazad-Dûm by calling himself a "servant of the Secret Fire" (II.v.322).

In imitation of Melkor, his foul lieutenant Sauron (who was once a member of a lesser order of Valar known as the Maiar) continues to use both darkness and fire as weapons to resist that Light that he is unable either to defeat or to understand. He is, on the one hand, what is popularly referred to as an evil genius, and yet, on the other, he is utterly myopic: both literally (he only has one eye) and figuratively (he lacks discernment). The only reason that Sam and Frodo are able to smuggle the One Ring into the heart of Mordor is because Sauron is incapable of perceiving that someone who possessed the Ring would seek to destroy it. As Gandalf explains to Aragorn, Sauron

> does not yet perceive [the Fellowship's] purpose clearly. He supposes that we were all going to Minas Tirith; for that is what he would himself have done in our place. . . . That we should wish to cast him down and have *no* one in his place is not a thought that occurs to his mind. That we should try to destroy the Ring itself has not yet entered into his darkest dream. (III.v.485–6)

The reason that Sauron has not guessed the true purpose of the Fellowship is not that he is a fool or even that he is prideful, but that he simply cannot conceive that someone would willingly forsake power. He is completely blind to the ways and motivations of goodness; such Light is too bright for his darkened eye to fathom.

In like manner, Gollum also cannot conceive that Frodo would destroy the Ring; if he had, he surely would not have led the Hobbits into Mordor. And Saruman, too, has his blind spots, bred by his own lost ability to gaze into the Light, to fathom the ways of goodness. Even as he stands defeated atop the pinnacle of Orthanc, he believes, irrationally, that Gandalf has some secret motive of his own for helping the free peoples of Middle-earth to defeat Sauron. He thinks that Gandalf shares his own perverse ambition to take the place of Sauron, and accuses him falsely of seeking for himself not only "the Keys of Barad-dûr itself . . . [but] the crowns of seven kings, and the rods of the Five Wizards" (III.x.569).

It is important to note that Saruman's accusation comes in the context of Gandalf's gracious offer to forgive Saruman his evil. But Saruman will have none of it; indeed, two more times near the end of the novel he will reject again a similar mercy offered to him first by Gandalf and Galadriel, and then later by Frodo. For mercy, too, is a kind of light that blinds and exposes, and the darkness cannot bear to have its own sins and corruptions revealed.

Light, like the Word of God (Hebrews 4:12), is a double-edged sword that cuts both ways, shattering those who resist it but healing those who embrace it. With a shaft of white light, Gandalf repels one of the Nazgûl, while Sam, with the light in the phial of Galadriel, blinds the eyes of Shelob and cuts through the filth and darkness of her lair. Later, as he makes his way toward the Tower of Cirith Ungol, where Frodo, recovered from Shelob's sting, is being held prisoner, Sam uses the phial again to protect himself from the Two Watchers who guard the Tower. Tolkien's description of the encounter between the pure Light and the perverse Watchers (who strongly resemble the vulture-headed god Tash in the Chronicles) captures powerfully the full force of John 1:5:

> [Sam] drew slowly out the phial of Galadriel and held it up.
> Its white light quickened swiftly, and the shadows under the
> dark arch fled. The monstrous Watchers sat there cold and still,
> revealed in all their hideous shape. For a moment Sam caught a
> glitter in the black stones of their eyes, the very malice of which
> made him quail; but slowly he felt their will waver and crumble
> into fear. (VI.1.882)

Evil fears the sword that might defeat it, but it fears even more
the light that reveals its true, hideous nature. Always it crum-
bles beneath the hot gaze of goodness as a prisoner does beneath
the merciless glare of the interrogation lamp. Perhaps following
Dante, who imprisons Satan in an ice block at the very bottom of
hell, Tolkien depicts Sauron as a beast who never leaves his lair
(he does the same for Morgoth in *The Silmarillion*). Ironically, for
all his attempts to imprison the peoples of Middle-earth, Sauron
is already a virtual prisoner in Barad-dûr. Isolated and barricaded
in his Dark Tower, the supposed Dark Lord (like the supposedly
invincible Shelob) crouches in perpetual fear of the Light that he
can never—and will never—understand.

DEAF TO ASLAN'S SONG

Like Tolkien, Lewis also presents us (in *The Magician's Nephew*)
with a set of dark and powerful villains who, like Sauron and
Shelob, fear the Light of goodness that they cannot understand.
In chapter 13, we discussed how Uncle Andrew and Queen Jadis
fit perfectly the type of the Byronic Hero who allows his Nietzs-
chean will to power to lead him into evil. In the second half of
the novel, during which Lewis describes the Creation of Narnia,

Andrew and Jadis appear again, this time as virtual embodiments of John 1:5.

As in Tolkien's *Ainulindale*, Lewis has his Creator (Aslan) sing Narnia into being, and, as in Tolkien as well, Aslan is joined in his song by angelic beings (stars in Lewis's case) who harmonize with the initial melody that proceeds alone out of the mind of Aslan. The song, and its creative power, is witnessed by two earth children (Digory and Polly), by a cabdriver (Frank) and his horse (Strawberry), and by Andrew and Jadis. The song, Lewis tells us,

> was, beyond comparison, the most beautiful noise [Digory] had ever heard. It was so beautiful he could hardly bear it. The horse seemed to like it too: he gave the sort of whinny a horse would give if, after years of being a cab-horse, it found itself back in the old field where it had played as a foal, and saw someone whom it remembered and loved coming across the field to bring it a lump of sugar.
>
> "Gawd!" said the Cabby. "Ain't it lovely. . . . I'd ha' been a better man all my life if I'd known there were things like this."
> (VIII.99–100)

To the heart willing to receive it, the song brings with it all that is most beautiful, most good, most alive. It is like light piercing through the darkness, awakening old desires for love, nurture, and goodness.

On Andrew and Jadis, however, whose occult studies and lust for power have severed them from the white light of truth and taught them the fear and dread of exposure, the song of Aslan provokes a far different response:

> The Cabby and the two children had open mouths and shining eyes; they were drinking in the sound, and they looked as

if it reminded them of something. Uncle Andrew's mouth was open too, but not open with joy. He looked more as if his chin had simply dropped away from the rest of his face. His shoulders were stooped and his knees shook. He was not liking the Voice. If he could have gotten away from it by creeping into a rat's hole, he would have done so. But the Witch looked as if, in a way, she understood the music better than any of them. Her mouth was shut, her lips were pressed together, and her fists were clenched. Ever since the song began she had felt that this whole world was filled with a Magic different from hers and stronger. She hated it. She would have smashed that whole world, or all worlds, to pieces, if it would only stop the singing. (VIII.100–1)

How tragic that the same song that brings such joy and wonder to Frank, Digory, and Polly is like poison to Andrew and Jadis. That which revives and restores the cabby and the children inspires in Andrew a desire to cower in fear and in Jadis a desire to resist and destroy. Despite their knowledge and practice of magic, neither can get inside the song (as the other four characters, including Strawberry, do), nor fathom its creative power. It is a mystery to them, but one they do not wish to solve or even study. In response to its overwhelming beauty, they can only conceive of two options: fight or flight. They are like the Dwarfs in the Stable in *The Last Battle* (see chapter 7) who refuse to see—and therefore cannot see—the glorious feast that Aslan lays out before them. In the hope of calming Andrew's fears, Aslan attempts to speak to him, but all Andrew can hear is the roar of a dumb beast. He is as deaf as he is blind to the light and goodness of Aslan's "white magic." He is a pitiable creature indeed.

But if Andrew (like Gollum and Wormtongue) is more pitiable

and pathetic, then Jadis (like Sauron and Saruman) is more to be hated and feared. Though she cannot understand the goodness of the song, she does recognize, as Andrew does not, how grave a threat it is to the type of power she desires. After attempting, unsuccessfully, to kill Aslan, she runs off into the northern climes of Narnia where she steals and eats an apple from a walled garden: an apple that grants her the gift of immortality. From the same tree, Digory plucks an apple but brings it back untasted to Aslan (as Aslan had commanded him to do). With the apple, Aslan plants a Tree of Protection to guard his new land of Narnia from Jadis. Aslan then explains to Digory that because Jadis has eaten the fruit "at the wrong time and in the wrong way," the smell of the Tree, "which is joy and life and health to you [will be] death and horror and despair to her" (XIV.173–4). Yes, the apple will provide her with "endless days like a goddess," but, Aslan adds solemnly, "length of days with an evil heart is only length of misery" (XIV.174).

Cut off as she is from the light, life, and joy of Aslan, Jadis's immortality can only bring her misery and despair. In the Christian worldview shared by Lewis and Tolkien, light equals life equals joy. As long as Jadis cannot understand the first, she cannot receive the other two.

CHAPTER SIXTEEN

EGYPTIAN ALLIANCES

As America and Britain fought for their lives against the tyranny of Hitler and the Nazis, they turned for aid to the Soviet Union of Stalin. Though it must be admitted that the alliance was all but forced on Roosevelt and Churchill, it turned out, in the end, to be a pact with the devil. Stalin, as the Western democracies slowly came to realize, was as brutal a dictator as Hitler, and Russian communism as evil a system as German fascism. Eastern Europe would pay dearly for our entangling alliance with the European equivalent of Mordor.

But then political expediency demanded the pact be made. After all, the reigning wisdom of the day asserted, the enemy of my enemy is my friend.

As proverbs go, this is most definitely *not* one to live one's life by.

So Israel found in the days after Solomon when the northern kingdom of Samaria and the southern kingdom of Judah were forced to negotiate and survive in a world of powerful and competing empires: Babylon, Assyria, Egypt. Again and again God warned His people to stay out of the struggles between these three heathen nations — to trust in Him, rather than Egypt, to protect them from Assyria and Babylon. First Isaiah, then Jeremiah, then Ezekiel issued their prophetic warning to the northern and southern kings:

> "Woe to the obstinate children," declares the Lord, "to those who carry out plans that are not mine, forming an alliance, but not by my Spirit, heaping sin upon sin; who go down to Egypt without consulting me; who look for help to Pharaoh's protection, to Egypt's shade for refuge. But Pharaoh's protection will be to your shame, Egypt's shade will bring you disgrace. (Isaiah 30:1–3 NIV)

> Then all who live in Egypt will know that I am the Lord. "You [Egypt] have been a staff of reed for the house of Israel. When they grasped you with their hands, you splintered and you tore open their shoulders; when they leaned on you, you broke and their backs were wrenched." (Ezekiel 29:6–7 NIV)

Egypt was Israel's oldest enemy, a power that had enslaved them for hundreds of years, and yet, when danger faced them from Assyria or Babylon, they turned to the chariots of Egypt rather than the mighty arm of the Lord to aid them. And no matter how often their pagan allies forsook and betrayed them (Egypt was not the only one), no matter how often the reed that they leaned on pierced their own flesh, they always returned with open arms.

Years before, the great Solomon had already compromised

the worship of Yahweh by marrying the daughter of Pharaoh and being swayed by her heathen idols. But then Egypt was glorious in her strength, riches, and splendor. She had survived and ruled for centuries untold, a thing, it seemed, of permanence. How could one go wrong if he trusted to such a power? How could he not benefit from harnessing the might of such an army? Israel was a godly nation, after all. She need not fear being corrupted by Egypt. On the contrary, perhaps God himself had meant for Samaria and Judah to seek such alliances: to convert the evil of Egypt into a force for good. What could be more noble than that?

TOO GREAT TO WIELD

At the Council of Elrond, Boromir voices precisely the arguments of the Israelites of old. When he realizes that Elrond means to destroy the Ring in the fires of Mount Doom, he is stirred to passion and speaks aloud his exasperation with the Council's seemingly irrational decision:

> I do not understand all this. . . . Saruman is a traitor, but did he not have a glimpse of wisdom? Why do you speak ever of hiding and destroying? Why should we not think that the Great Ring has come into our hands to serve us in the very hour of need? Wielding it the Free Lords of the Free may surely defeat the Enemy. That is what he most fears, I deem.
>
> The Men of Gondor are valiant, and they will never submit; but they may be beaten down. Valour needs first strength, and then a weapon. Let the Ring be your weapon, if it has such power as you say. (II.ii.260–1)

It is significant that Boromir takes his cue from the actions of Saruman, who has been exerting all his power and influence to secure the Ring for himself. Boromir feels certain that he and the Men of Gondor can walk in the footsteps of Saruman's "wisdom" without being corrupted by his lust and pride. He thinks they can wield the power of the Enemy for the sake of good, that they can make a pact with the devil and then find a loophole.

Elrond gently rebukes Boromir for his folly:

> Alas, no. . . . We cannot use the Ruling Ring. That we now know too well. It belongs to Sauron and was made by him alone, and is altogether evil. Its strength, Boromir, is too great for anyone to wield at will, save only those who have already a great power of their own. But for them it holds an even deadlier peril. The very desire of it corrupts the heart. Consider Saruman. If any of the Wise should with this Ring overthrow the Lord of Mordor, using his own arts, he would then set himself on Sauron's throne, and yet another Dark Lord would appear. And that is another reason why the Ring should be destroyed: as long as it is in the world it will be a danger even to the Wise. For nothing is evil in the beginning. Even Sauron was not so. (II.ii.261)

I have already quoted the last two sentences of Elrond's speech in chapter 14 to emphasize Tolkien's central belief that evil people are actually good people who have gone bad. Viewed in their fuller context, the words of Elrond can now be seen to represent a warning as well as a theological principle: if even Saruman can be led astray by his "Egyptian alliance" with Mordor and the One Ring, then so can anyone, small or great, human or Elf, simple or wise. A bow, a lance, a dagger, an axe: all of these are neutral objects that can be used for good or for evil. But not the One Ring. The Ring is simply and wholly evil; one cannot use it without being corrupted by it. Even Gandalf and Galadriel do not trust themselves with the Ring.

Caution: Elrond's words should not be misinterpreted as a blanket condemnation of war: neither Tolkien nor Lewis was a pacifist. The taking up of arms does not, in and of itself, corrupt us, but only the lusting for it and the pride (and folly) that drives us to win the battle at all costs, no matter what principles must be compromised or methods must be used. Faramir understands this well and swears before Frodo and Sam that he would not use, or even touch, the Ring "if it lay by the highway. Not were Minas Tirith falling in ruin and I alone could save her, so, using the weapon of the Dark Lord for her good and my glory" (IV.v.656). What then does Faramir want? Is he an idealistic pacifist? a naïve escapist? He is neither. He will fight if he must, but to restore Gondor to its former glory, not to transform her into another Mordor:

> I would see the White Tree in flower again in the courts of the
> kings, and the Silver Crown return, and Minas Tirith in peace:
> Minas Anor again as of old, full of light, high and fair, beautiful
> as a queen among other queens: not a mistress of many slaves,
> nay, not even a kind mistress of willing slaves. War must be,
> while we defend our lives against a destroyer who would devour
> all; but I do not love the bright sword for its sharpness, nor
> the arrow for its swiftness, nor the warrior for his glory. I love
> only that which they defend: the city of the Men of Númenor;
> and I would have her loved for her memory, her ancientry, her
> beauty, and her present wisdom. Not feared, save as men may
> fear the dignity of a man, old and wise. (IV.v.656)

If this be escapism, then we could use a great deal more of it in our world. Faramir (who has learned at the feet of Gandalf) understands, as his brother did not, the inherent contradiction in any policy that would do evil that good might result (see Romans 3:8). He knows that when we make the enemy of our enemy into our friend, we risk becoming the enemy ourselves: risk making a desert and calling it a peace. When war and power are made ends in themselves, instead of means to a higher end, they corrupt the souls not only of the warriors but of the citizens for whom they claim to be fighting. It converts their city into an armed camp, as cruel and slavish-minded as the camp of the evil enemy.

To win such a war is to lose it even before it is begun.

TOO DEAR A PRICE

In the previous chapter, we quoted Aslan's words to Digory concerning the relationship between the now-immortal Jadis and the Tree of Protection. Because Jadis stole and ate an apple in defiance of Aslan, she now cannot bear the smell of life and goodness that proceeds from the Tree—even though that Tree was grown from an apple identical to the one eaten by Jadis. But this is not all that Aslan has to tell Digory concerning that Tree which he helped to plant. If, Aslan explains,

> any Narnian, unbidden, had stolen an apple and planted it here to protect Narnia, it would have protected Narnia. But it would have done so by making Narnia into another strong and cruel empire like Charn [Jadis's former kingdom], not the kindly land I mean it to be. (XIV.175)

It would have become, that is to say, what Gondor would have become had Faramir (or Boromir, or Denethor) used the Ring to defeat Sauron and Mordor: a mistress of many slaves. Both the stolen apple and the Ring *work*: they *do* give the immortality and the power that they promise, just as the forbidden fruit in Genesis 3 *does* open the eyes of Adam and Eve to the knowledge of good and evil. The lie does not lurk in the primary promise of life-strength-wisdom, but in the accompanying, deceptive promise that these things, once achieved, will make one into a god: eternal, omnipotent, omniscient. The lie rests in the false promise that the life it gives will be a life worth living, the strength a strength worth wielding, the wisdom a wisdom worth possessing.

When Digory plucks the apple and prepares to take it back to Aslan, Jadis tempts him (unsuccessfully) to keep the apple and to use it to restore the health of his mother (who is dying back in England). Accordingly, after telling Digory what would have happened had a Narnian planted the Tree of Protection, Aslan goes on to tell him what would have happened had Digory taken Jadis's advice and used the apple, unlawfully if unselfishly, to heal his mother:

> "Understand, then, that it would have healed her; but not to your joy or hers. The day would have come when both you and she would have looked back and said it would have been better to die in that illness."
>
> And Digory . . . [realized then] that there might be things more terrible even than losing someone you love by death.
> (XIV.175)

Both Lewis and Tolkien knew that there *are* things worse than death, than pain, than defeat, even if our age has forgotten it. They knew that there are forms of life and health and victory that can be bought at too dear a price.

NIKABRIK'S FOLLY

For nearly a thousand years, the Tree of Protection keeps Jadis's evil at bay, although she eventually (in the guise of the White

Witch) seizes Narnia and holds her in a century-long winter. With the help of Peter, Susan, Edmund, and Lucy, Aslan defeats the White Witch and provides Narnia with another millennia of relative peace and prosperity. That is, until the Telmarines seize control of Narnia and drive the talking animals underground. In the midst, however, of the tyranny of King Miraz, a strong but gentle-hearted prince arises who yearns for the old Narnia with the same fervor that Faramir yearns for the old Gondor. His name, of course, is Prince Caspian, and he (like Faramir) is willing to give his life in battle if it will help to restore the glory that has been lost. But he will not do so by any means necessary.

In this, he is markedly different from Nikabrik, a Machiavellian Dwarf who knows how to play the game of realpolitik and who believes firmly that the enemy of his enemy is his friend. In a dark and lurid scene guaranteed to chill the blood of the reader, Nikabrik tries to convince Caspian to seek a different kind of aid than Aslan and the earth children to help him in his war against Miraz. Aslan, Nikabrik claims, is either not on their side or does not have the power to save them from the Telmarines. But there is another power, Nikabrik suggests, that can: "'I mean a power so much greater than Aslan's that it held Narnia spellbound for years and years if the stories are true'" (XII.162). With horror, Caspian realizes that Nikabrik is referring to the White Witch, she who was as great an enemy to Narnia as Egypt was to Israel.

> "Yes," said Nikabrik very slowly and distinctly, "I mean the Witch. Sit down again. Don't all take fright at a name as if you were children. We want power: and we want a power that will be on our side. As for power, do not the stories say that the Witch defeated Aslan, and bound him and killed him . . ." (XII.162–3)

Caspian immediately responds that Aslan rose again from the dead and defeated the Witch, but Nikabrik casts doubt on the faith of Caspian and his loyal followers. After all, did not Aslan disappear shortly after his "supposed" resurrection? "But it's very different with the Witch. They say she ruled for a hundred years: a hundred years of winter. There's power, if you like. There's something practical." To which Caspian replies:

> "But, heaven and earth! . . . Haven't we always been told that she was the worst enemy of all? Wasn't she a tyrant ten times worse than Miraz?"
>
> "Perhaps," said Nikabrik in a cold voice. "Perhaps she *was* for you humans, if there were any of you in those days."
> (XII.163–4)

Prince Caspian may be a fairy tale written for children, but in this scene, Lewis offers a critique of political (and moral) expediency that is as sharp as Plato or Thucydides.

Power, they say, corrupts, and absolute power corrupts absolutely. Like Saruman and Boromir, Nikabrik has so blinded himself that he is ready to make a pact with Narnia's oldest, darkest enemy if it will help him achieve his goals. Faith, truth, goodness are inconsequential. There is only power: raw, naked power. To it and for it he has (like Faust) surrendered his soul.

in DEFENSE
of STORIES

In addition to *The Silmarillion*, *The Hobbit*, and *The Lord of the Rings*, Tolkien also published a number of short stories that sweep their readers away to the world of faerie. All are well worth reading and offer a lighter, more frothy complement to the grand and weighty themes of *The Lord of the Rings*. However, there is one story whose lightness belies its more serious undertones. That story is "Leaf by Niggle," and its "seriousness" comes from the fact that it is strongly autobiographical—that it offers, in fact, an apologia or defense for the time and energy Tolkien devoted to constructing his mythic world of Middle-earth.

The hero of the tale is a little man named Niggle who loves to paint leaves. Indeed, he spends so much of his day "niggling" away at his leaves that he has been unable to fulfill his great aspiration: "to paint a whole tree, with all of its leaves in the same style, and all of them different." During the course of the narrative, Niggle goes on a strange journey which, the reader slowly comes to realize, is really a journey through purgatory. At the end, as he approaches heaven, he sees the Tree he had so long desired to paint, its leaves opened to the breeze, its branches bending and swaying in the wind. It is the real Tree of which his earthly dabblings and nigglings were but shadows and glimpses. It is the greater sub-creation, the complete Middle-earth that Tolkien would have given us had his time been unlimited and his vision perfect.

But the story does not end there. It ends back on the earth, with a group of Niggle's neighbors discussing their thoughts about the deceased painter's contributions to society. The most cynical (and pragmatic) of them, Tompkins the Councillor, has this to say:

> Of course, painting has uses. . . . But you couldn't make use of his painting. There is plenty of scope for bold young men not afraid of new ideas and new methods. None for this old-fashioned stuff. Private day-dreaming. He could not have designed a telling poster to save his life. Always fiddling with leaves and flowers. I asked him why, once. He said he thought they were pretty! Can you believe it? He said *pretty*! "What, digestive and genital organs of plants?" I said to him; and he had nothing to answer. Silly footler.

There were many in Tolkien's day—and many still today—who felt exactly that way about *The Lord of the Rings*. Why should a highly educated Oxford don waste his time spinning fairy stories and creating unreal worlds? Could he not find a more practical, socially responsible way of using his talents?

I am one reader—and there are millions of others!—who feels particularly grateful that Tolkien (and Lewis) used his gifts in exactly the way that he did. The stories that Tolkien and Lewis spin are pretty, yes; old-fashioned, yes; the fruit of private daydreams, yes. But they are also stories that have vastly enriched an age that so desperately needed them. All ages at all times need stories, but ours needs them so much more. True, of entertainment, and even of fantasy, we have no lack. But we are starved for the kind of stories that will supply us with the fullness offered so freely in the Chronicles and *The Lord of the Rings*. The stories that we need are precisely those that will beckon us to follow their heroes along the Road; that will embody for us the true nature of good and evil, virtue and vice, and then challenge us to engage in the struggle between the two; that will open our eyes and ears to that sacramental faerie magic that we so often miss.

In chapter 9, I quoted Lewis's claim (in *The Four Loves*) that though friendship may have no "survival value," it lends "value to survival." The same may be said — emphatically said — about stories. We can exist without them, but what an impoverished existence it will be. Stories add spice to the often bland fare of living, and a dash of fairy dust to what otherwise is tedious and mundane. And, if Tolkien and Lewis are right, they will persist even beyond the grave. Thus does Lewis end the last chapter of his last Chronicle with an affirmation and a celebration of the eternal endurance of stories:

> And for us this is the end of all the stories, and we can most truly say that they all lived happily ever after. But for them it was only the beginning of the real story. All their life in this world and all their adventures in Narnia had only been the cover and the title page: now at last they were beginning Chapter One of the Great Story, which no one on earth has read: which goes on for ever: in which every chapter is better than the one before. (*The Last Battle*, XVI.184)

To read, to enjoy, to love the tales of Narnia and Middle-earth may do more than guide and please us on our earthly pilgrimage. It may, who knows, prepare us as well for the life to come.

Let us begin.

TOLKIEN *and* MIDDLE-EARTH: A BIBLIOGRAPHICAL ESSAY

BIOGRAPHIES OF TOLKIEN

The essential starting place for a study of J. R. R. Tolkien is *Tolkien* by Humphrey Carpenter (first published in 1977 by George Allen & Unwin). This book is heralded on the cover as the "authorized biography," not as some sham publishing ploy, but because it is, in fact, the authorized biography. Carpenter was given complete access to the Tolkien family and letters and has used this access judiciously and skillfully. He gives a fair and well-rounded portrait of the author of *The Lord of the Rings* (henceforth,

LOTR) that gets to the heart of the man without subjecting him to any trendy psychoanalysis or hero worship. The book keeps the focus on Tolkien rather than his works, but it nevertheless manages to offer some brief but insightful analysis of Tolkien's fiction as well.

Carpenter followed up his biography by publishing (with the close assistance of Christopher Tolkien, the son who was most involved in his father's work and who would do the world a great service by editing for publication *The Silmarillion*) a truly magisterial edition of *The Letters of J. R. R. Tolkien* (George Allen & Unwin, 1981; available in a 2000 high-quality paperback from Houghton Mifflin). Anyone who wants to understand the loves, hopes, and beliefs of the man who created what many polls have called the book of the century, simply *must* skim through—if not indeed read all—of these remarkable letters. Of special interest are a whole series of letters he wrote to Christopher during World War II that reveal Tolkien's complex view of war and how it all links up with LOTR which, though it is not an allegory, does embody the spirit of the times (these same set of letters were written simultaneously with Tolkien's writing of most of LOTR). The later letters are essential for fans of LOTR as they document Tolkien's own long and winding meditations on the theme and message of his great epic—many in answer to letters written him by inquiring fans. Tolkien the devout Catholic and loving husband and father also emerges from these letters in a touchingly human way.

Speaking of Tolkien's deep Catholic faith, it should be noted that though Carpenter is fair and balanced in his discussion of Tolkien's Christian beliefs, he ultimately does not devote quite as much time as he should to this essential aspect of Tolkien and his work. Readers who wish to explore further Tolkien's faith and its impact on his life and writings are urged to read *Tolkien: Man and Myth* by Joseph Pearce (Ignatius Press, 1998). Pearce, partly through a close meditation on Tolkien's letters, helps us to understand the role that Catholicism and the Catholic Church played in Tolkien's life, and why we cannot fully appreciate the scope and worldview of LOTR without recourse to Catholic Christian thought. Pearce's very readable book is also of note as its first chapter offers an entertaining if troubling overview of the negative reaction on the part of the literati to the designation of LOTR as the book of the century.

This negative reaction is also documented in the foreword to T. A. Shippey's *J. R. R. Tolkien: Author of the Century* (Houghton Mifflin, 2000), a book which opens up and expands on the fine work Shippey had done earlier in his *The Road to Middle-Earth* (Houghton Mifflin, 1982, with a second edition from Grafton in 1992). The earlier work, as its title suggests, takes us through the many influences that led up to LOTR, while the later work offers a fuller close reading of *The Hobbit*, LOTR, *The Silmarillion*, and the shorter fiction. Both books put a heavy emphasis on philology, not surprising as Shippey holds the Chair of English Language and Medieval Literature at Leeds once held by Tolkien himself. The focus on linguistic concerns makes Shippey's books a bit more specialized; still, he does his best to cast them in laymen terms, and the dedicated reader who knows little of philology will come away richer for the experience. After all, as Carpenter and Tolkien's other biographers accurately point out, the languages of the various races of Middle-earth preceded (and birthed) the creation of Middle-earth itself, and *not* vice versa. As such, Shippey's focus on philology is by no means misplaced or overworked. Language lies at the heart of LOTR. Though the focus of this essay is on books accessible to the general reader, I mention Shippey not only because of the centrality of his work on Tolkien but because I believe he comes within the ambit, if on the margins, of the general reader. Two other authors who lie on the margin but which may appeal to those seeking a challenge are Verlyn Flieger (*Splintered Light: Logos and Language in Tolkien's World*) and Jane Chance (*Tolkien and the Invention of Myth*).

Before turning to the LOTR itself, I would like to add a few more books that fall into the biographical category. First, those who wish a readable and fairly brief complement to Carpenter's *Tolkien* might enjoy Daniel Grotta's *J. R. R. Tolkien: Architect of Middle Earth*. Second, those who wish to explore the friendship of Lewis and Tolkien and their participation in the Inklings (a friendship and a literary club that were both essential to the genesis of LOTR and the Chronicles of Narnia), absolutely *must* read Carpenter's *The Inklings: C. S. Lewis, J. R. R. Tolkien, Charles Williams, and Their Friends* (Houghton Mifflin, 1979). This well-conceived book provides its reader with the rare opportunity to eavesdrop on three great minds as they encourage and critique one another. It also offers, in the last chapter, a hypothetical meeting of the Inklings, pieced together from clues found in the letters and works of Lewis, Tolkien, and the other Inklings. Those interested in a more detailed study of how the Inklings both supported and critiqued each other's work must consult Diana Glyer's carefully researched *The Company They Keep: C. S. Lewis and J. R. R. Tolkien as Writers in Community* (Kent State University Press, 2008). Finally, those wishing to explore even further the Lewis-Tolkien friendship should consult *Tolkien and C. S. Lewis: The Gift of Friendship* (HiddenSpring, 2003) by Colin Duriez, a respected, oft-interviewed scholar of both men, who has also written the helpful *Tolkien and the Lord of the Rings: A Guide to Middle-Earth* (HiddenSpring, 2001).

TOLKIEN'S FICTION

As mentioned in the introduction, my preferred text of LOTR is the one-volume edition first printed in Great Britain by Harper-Collins Publishers in 1994 and reprinted in America by Houghton Mifflin Company (available not only in paperback and hardcover but in several special collector's editions). But there are, of course, numerous editions of every shape, size, and price available, including ones published in the 1990s by Houghton Mifflin that feature beautiful and haunting illustrations by Alan Lee (these editions make nice gift books). The one-volume edition mentioned above is also available as three separate books (as Unwin first published them in the 1950s); what is nice, though, about these books is that the publishers wisely keyed the pagination to reflect that of the one-volume edition (thus *The Two Towers* does not begin on page 1, but on page 403). Although those wishing to read LOTR casually during a trip might prefer to read it as three separate books (it is less bulky that way), those who intend to do a close, annotated reading of the epic are strongly encouraged to purchase the one-volume edition to allow for the taking of cross-referenced notes. LOTR is best and most profitably read as one book—as Tolkien originally intended it to be—rather than as a trilogy.

There are as many editions of *The Hobbit* as there are of LOTR. I myself prefer the high-quality paperback put out by Houghton Mifflin in the late '90s that includes all the original illustrations drawn by Tolkien himself. As for *The Silmarillion*, I would encourage a hardcover edition, as it offers much wider margins for taking notes and includes a fuller and larger map, which is very helpful when trying to piece together the action. Fans who wish to explore further Tolkien's grander conception of Middle-earth have a plethora of other books to choose from, all edited (like *The Silmarillion*) by Christopher Tolkien in the years following the death of his father. The three most helpful—which are available in both hardcover and paperback, though the latter have exceedingly narrow margins—are *The Book of Lost Tales, Part I, The Book of Lost Tales, Part II*, and *Unfinished Tales*. For the fan who must read absolutely everything, Christopher Tolkien followed up Parts I and II of *The Book of Lost Tales* with another dozen or so volumes, all of which make up collectively The History of Middle-Earth.

Fans of Tolkien will be particularly happy to know that in 2002 The Quality Paper Book Club of New York put out a collection of Tolkien's shorter works titled *A Tolkien Miscellany*. This edition not only includes the full texts of (and original illustrations for) "Smith of Wooton Major," "Farmer Giles of Ham," and "The Adventures of Tom Bombadil," but the full texts of "On Fairy-Stories," "Leaf by Niggle," and Tolkien's translations of and notes for *Sir Gawain and the Green Knight*, *Pearl*, and *Sir Orfeo*. This well-made but inexpensive collection belongs on the shelf of every Tolkien lover.

There are many guides out there to Middle-earth, but the one that is most essential is *The Complete Guide to Middle-Earth: Tolkien's World from A to Z* by Robert Foster (which has gone through many editions since 1971 and is currently available from Ballantine Books). This incredibly thorough encyclopedia more than lives up to its title and will help the lost reader navigate his way through all of Tolkien's works that relate to Middle-earth. Readers who have not yet made their way through *The Silmarillion* will particularly appreciate the way Foster's guide fills in all the gaps. Another excellent guide is J. E. A. Tyler's *The Complete Tolkien Companion* (first published in 1976 by Pan Books, but available in numerous editions). A third guide that, to me at least, is indispensable is *The Atlas of Middle-Earth* by Karen Wynn Fonstad (Houston Mifflin, 1991, revised edition). This nicely laid out book offers maps that cover the full range of the history of Middle-earth; it is particularly helpful in illustrating those parts of *The Silmarillion* that are not covered by the maps provided by Christopher Tolkien.

There are many, many books out there that offer both overviews and deeper analyses of LOTR. I will list below three recent studies that I found the most helpful both for my own understanding of Tolkien's epic and in terms of my own writing of this book. I have chosen these three in particular because they show the most sensitivity to the essentially Christian worldview that underlies LOTR without simply turning Tolkien's subcreation into a hidden Christian allegory. The first, that is by no means as trendy as its title suggests, is *The Gospel According to Tolkien: Visions of the Kingdom in Middle-earth* by Ralph Wood (Westminster John Knox Press, 2003). Wood does a wonderful job analyzing the role of providence in LOTR as well as the more general moral vision that underlies Tolkien's epic. As I do in this book, Wood puts a great emphasis on the cardinal and theological virtues and also speaks at length about friendship. In structuring my book, I did not consciously intend to imitate Wood's structure; still, it must be conceded that Wood's study precedes my own. In many ways, our handling of the virtues overlaps for the same reason that LOTR and Wagner's *Ring* overlap: Professor Wood and I are both imbibing at the same traditional well. In my case, the fact that my three greatest influences are Plato, Dante, and C. S. Lewis (who covers the seven virtues in *Mere Christianity*) almost guaranteed that I would take up the virtues in my study. I find it refreshing that though both Professor Wood and I teach at Baptist Universities (he at Baylor University and I at Houston Baptist University), our focus on the seven virtues puts us more in company with the Catholic vision of Tolkien.

The second book, and one that offers perhaps the finest chapter-by-chapter analysis of LOTR, is *The Battle for Middle-earth: Tolkien's Divine Design in The Lord of the Rings* by Fleming Rutledge (Eerdmans, 2004). Rutledge guides us effortlessly through the complex twists and turns of Tolkien's plot, revealing for us as we go how grace underlies the actions of all the characters. For my taste, Rutledge overemphasizes "predestination" over "free will" (had I not known better, I would have pegged her as a Calvinist minister rather than an Episcopalian priest); still, she backs up her argument with copious references to the text and Tolkien's letters, and she does a powerful job analyzing Tolkien's constant use of the passive voice to suggest that a will deeper than that of the characters is impelling the action. Rutledge also weaves into her study some particularly good commentary on the film version directed by Peter Jackson.

Third, I would highly recommend a brief but thought-provoking study published in England: *Secret Fire: The Spiritual Vision of J. R. R. Tolkien* by Stratford Caldecott (Darton, Longman, and Todd, 2003). Caldecott, the director of the Chesterton Institute for Faith & Culture in Oxford, opens up for us the rich Catholic vision of Tolkien's epic in a way that is revelatory rather than preachy. The yearning for light and transcendence, the role of the good, the true, and the beautiful, healing and renewal: all come alive in his carefully nuanced analysis of LOTR. Caldecott has also done, to my mind, the best job of assessing fully the role that the Virgin

Mary plays in LOTR, and enabling non-Catholics to appreciate that role.

Four final books that are worth a look are *J. R. R. Tolkien's Sanctifying Myth: Understanding Middle Earth* by Bradley J. Birzer (ISI Books, 2002), *Master of Middle-earth: The Fiction of J. R. R. Tolkien* by Paul H. Kocher (Houghton Mifflin, 1972), *Tolkien: A Celebration*, edited by Joseph Pearce (Ignatius Press, 1999), and *Tolkien and the Critics: Essays on J. R. R. Tolkien's The Lord of the Rings*, edited by Neil D. Isaacs and Rose A. Zimbardo (University of Notre Dame Press, 1968); in 2004, Isaacs and Zimbardo put out a second collection of essays, *Understanding the Lord of the Rings: The Best of Tolkien Criticism* (Houghton Mifflin).

TOLKIEN IN RADIO, TV, AND FILM

In 1981, Brian Sibley adapted LOTR into a 13-part radio play for the BBC that can be purchased on cassette or CD. The adaptation is excellent and features Ian Holm as Frodo (who, ironically, plays Bilbo in the Peter Jackson film), Michael Hordern as Gandalf, and Robert Stephens as Aragorn. The series omits (wisely, I think) the entire Tom Bombadil episode from Book I, and it intercuts (again wisely) the actions of Books III/IV and Books V/VI; however, aside from these changes, the adaptation is a close and faithful one with excellent casting and music and a fine narration by Gerard Murphy. I would highly recommend purchasing the series and listening to it with your family during long car trips (as I have done, with much success, with my own family). LOTR was later adapted again for American radio, but this version lacks both the force and the magic of the BBC version. The entire LOTR is also available read aloud (masterfully) by Rob Inglis (www.recordedbooks.com).

In 1978, Ralph Bakshi put out an animated film version of the first half of LOTR that makes use of an odd animation style that mixes drawings and the use of live actors. Though somewhat interesting, the film fails to capture the scope or richness of the novel. (A Rankin-Bass animated version of *The Hobbit* made for TV in 1977 was far more successful; though the budget is small, the movie nevertheless captures much of the magic of the novel.)

The unfortunate failure of Bakshi's film seemed to shut the door on any hope of a full screen version, until, to the great delight of the majority of Tolkien lovers, Peter Jackson released (in three successive years: 2001–3) his intensely imaginative and powerful trilogy of films. Speaking as an English professor who also teaches film, I consider Jackson's trilogy to be a complete success and a triumph of screen art. The script, the casting, the acting, the music, the direction, the cinematography, the sets and costumes — everything about this film is superb and, as far as I am concerned, a worthy tribute to Tolkien's epic. (To ask whether Tolkien would have liked the film is irrelevant; among the few failings of Tolkien — and Lewis — was his complete lack of appreciation for or understanding of the medium of film.)

Like the BBC radio series, the films omit the Tom Bombadil episode and intercut the separate trajectories of the Fellowship after it breaks up at the end of Book II. Though the first film stays fairly close to the novel, the second and third films indulge in some major rearrangements of episodes, and even add in some elements that violate some major parts of the novel: the Elves come to the rescue at the Battle of Helms Deep; tension is put between Rohan and Gondor that is not there in the novel; Merry and Pippin become the main instigators in convincing the Ents to attack; the post-possessed Theoden is shown to be weaker than in the novel; Gimli is treated as a more comic figure, etc. To the dismay of many fans, the entire episode of the Scouring of the Shire is omitted, though I would argue that this decision was necessary given the type of plot structure demanded by the medium of feature film making. The needs of the genre also demanded an expansion of the Aragorn-Arwen love story—though the filmmakers borrowed much of their plotting for this expansion from the appendices to LOTR. As far as I am concerned, however, none of these changes, or the several others not mentioned, compromises the basic thrust of Tolkien's vision. Indeed, the film intensifies much of the drama and tightens up much that is arguably slack in the novel. All the characters (especially Gollum) are brought vividly to life, and Middle-earth comes alive in a way that I did not think possible to achieve. To my mind, the only serious failing of the film (and many would agree with me here) is in its characterization of Faramir—who is a far more noble and interesting character in the book than he is in the films.

Fans of LOTR should not only watch these films again and again, but really must purchase or at least borrow the special extended DVD editions of each of the three films. All the extra scenes included on the DVDs are worth viewing as is most (if not all) of the extra material. Along with the fascinating documentaries on the making of the films—that include spectacular footage of all the original New Zealand locations and how they were converted into the many locales of LOTR—each of the three special editions includes a separate documentary on Tolkien and his writing of the novel and on the process by which the book was converted into a screenplay. These documentaries are well-produced and scripted and include interviews with many Tolkien experts. They are a must-see for Tolkien fans.

Finally, a suggestion. On one magical New Year's Eve, my family and I gathered our friends at our home at about 2:00 p.m., and watched, straight through, all three films in their extended editions (close to twelve hours of screen time). The experience was overwhelming—indeed, cathartic—and stayed with us for several days. For the first time, I truly *felt* what Tolkien meant by the eucatastrophe. I would highly recommend repeating this experience with your own friends and family.

LEWIS *and* NARNIA: A BIBLIOGRAPHICAL ESSAY

BIOGRAPHIES OF LEWIS

There are even more biographies out there of Lewis than of Tolkien. The first to appear was *C. S. Lewis: A Biography* by Roger Lancelyn Green and Walter Hooper (Macmillan, 1974). Both men knew Lewis during his lifetime: the former was a pupil and friend and a well-known children's writer (he suggested to Lewis the series title of Chronicles of Narnia); the latter was Lewis's personal secretary during the last months of his life and has edited most of Lewis's essays and letters. Indeed, one of the helpful aspects of this biography is that it incorporates so many of Lewis's letters, diaries, and other personal writings. It offers a fine, rounded sense of the man, but it avoids touchy subjects and tends toward hagiography.

At the opposite end of the spectrum is A. N. Wilson's *C. S. Lewis: A Biography* (Fawcett Columbine, 1990). Wilson consciously sets out to dispel the Lewis-as-saint approach that Green and Hooper adopt in their biography, and, though he never quite descends to scandal or muckraking, his book tends to hold the core Lewis at arm's length. The main problem here is that Wilson has an obvious distaste for Lewis's brand of Christian apologetics, a distaste that leads him both to distort and misunderstand Lewis's Christian writings and to attempt psychological explanations for Lewis's religious beliefs. Still, it is good to be reminded that Lewis had his flaws and that he wasn't always as congenial as we like to imagine him; it is also good to remember that, even if Wilson *is* prejudiced against Lewis the apologist, so were many of Lewis's colleagues and fellow Inklings.

In between these two books comes a third that, to my mind, is the finest available biography of Lewis: *Jack: A Life of C. S. Lewis* by George Sayer (Crossway Books, 1994; originally published in 1988 under the title, *Jack: C. S. Lewis and His Times*). Like Green, Sayer was a one-time pupil and longtime friend of C. S. Lewis. His book combines the personal insight of the Green/Hooper biography with the critical objectivity of the Wilson biography. He is more frank and open about Lewis's struggles than Green/Hooper while yet refraining (as Wilson does not) from simplistic, reductive Freudian readings of his religious work. Readers will find particularly helpful Sayer's lengthy bibliography of works by and about Lewis. I would encourage those who have only seen the 1988 edition of Sayer's work to consult the afterword to the 1994 edition: here Sayer persuasively refutes Wilson's controversial contention that Lewis and Joy had sexual relations between their civil and church weddings; here also he defends Lewis in general against revisionist attacks on his character and his psyche.

Most recently, Alan Jacobs has given us *The Narnian: The Life and Imagination of C. S. Lewis* (HarperSanFrancisco, 2005). Jacobs's excellent and well-researched biography gives us more critical insight into Lewis's academic works than do the other bios, and he focuses especially on those events in Lewis's life that most influenced his writing of the Chronicles. Jacobs convincingly argues that it is the imaginative side of Lewis that gives us the key to his multifaceted character. Jacobs does a good job defending Lewis from many of Wilson's critiques, but he has a disturbing (and trendy) tendency to downplay Lewis the apologist and to "over apologize" for Lewis's supposed sexism. Still, lovers of Lewis and of the Chronicles should read this finely nuanced biography.

Lewis wrote his own spiritual autobiography that needs to be read by anyone wishing to understand Lewis: *Surprised by Joy*. He also wrote an allegorical autobiography of his spiritual journey titled *The Pilgrim's Regress* that is fascinating but very obscure to modern readers. If you wish to read this one, I would save it for last!

To gain deeper insight into Lewis's late marriage to Joy Davidman Gresham (and her subsequent death three years later: a tragic loss that inspired Lewis's book *A Grief Observed*), the best resources are Brian Sibley's *C. S. Lewis Through the Shadowlands: The Story of His Life with Joy Davidman* (Baker, 1994) and Douglas H. Gresham's *Lenten Lands: My Childhood with Joy Davidman and C. S. Lewis* (Harper & Row, 1994). The latter book was written by Joy's youngest son and is a moving and well-written document. The former was originally published in 1985 as a companion to the BBC TV-movie *Shadowlands* that tells the story of Lewis's marriage. This tender and beautiful film was later remade as a major motion picture (same title) directed by Richard Attenborough and starring Anthony Hopkins as Lewis and Debra Winger as Joy. Both films deserve multiple viewings.

For a more personal look at C. S. Lewis the man, I would urge you to pick up a copy of James T. Como's *C. S. Lewis at the Breakfast Table and Other Reminiscences* (Macmillan, 1979), which includes a smorgasbord of essays written by those who knew Lewis best. For a glimpse into Lewis's early, pre-Christian years (he did not become a believer until age thirty-two), you might consult Lewis's diaries—*All My Road before Me: The Diary of C. S. Lewis (1922–1927)*—or, even better, a large and revealing set of letters sent by Lewis to one of his oldest and closest friends: *They Stand Together: The Letters of C. S. Lewis to Arthur Greeves, 1914–1963*, edited by Walter Hooper (Collins, 1979). Lewis's brother, W. H. Lewis, published (in 1966) an edition of the *Letters of C. S. Lewis*; however, these have been superseded by a multivolume edition of the letters (*The Collected Letters of C. S. Lewis*) that Hooper has been editing for the last several years. Three of the best picture books that give a rich sense of Lewis's world are Clyde S. Kilby and Douglas Gilbert's *C. S. Lewis: Images of His World* (Eerdmans, 1973), Hooper's *Through Joy and Beyond: A Pictorial Biography of C. S. Lewis* (Macmillan, 1982), and Harry Lee Poe's *The Inklings of Oxford* (Zondervan, 2009). More recently, John Ryan Duncan has written *The Magic Never Ends: The Life and Works of C. S. Lewis* (W Publishing Group, 2001), which offers a simple but beguiling overview that is richly illustrated. There are also numerous anthologies of Lewis available, some of which offer complete works and others of which offer select passages grouped together thematically; the most fun is *The Quotable Lewis*, edited by

Wayne Martindale and Jerry Root.

If you begin to study Lewis in earnest, you will find that essentially everything Lewis ever wrote, from the earliest juvenilia to letters he wrote to children to the most obscure essays, has been published, usually under the able editorship of Hooper. Lewis's first childhood attempt at fashioning a fantasyland has even been published under the title *Boxen*. A good resource for all things Lewis is Hooper's *C. S. Lewis: A Companion and Guide* (Harper & Row, 1996). I would also (humbly, I hope!) highlight a twelve-lecture series I produced with The Teaching Company (1-800-TEACH12; www.teach12.com) that is titled *The Life and Writings of C. S. Lewis* (2000). The series covers Lewis's life and the full breadth of his work (over forty books and numerous essays); it also includes a course guide with an extensive annotated bibliography of works by and about Lewis. I have also written *Lewis Agonistes: How C. S. Lewis Can Train Us to Wrestle with the Modern and Postmodern World* (Broadman & Holman, 2003), which includes chapters on the new age and the arts that discuss the Chronicles at some length, and *Restoring Beauty: The Good, the True, and the Beautiful in the Writings of C. S. Lewis* (IVP Books, 2010), which offers analyses not only of the Chronicles but of Lewis's other four novels. Finally, I would invite you to visit my personal webpage (www.Loumarkos.com) where you can download for free numerous essays I've written on Lewis and related topics.

As I mentioned in my bibliography for Tolkien (appendix A), those wishing to explore the personal and literary friendship between Lewis and Tolkien should consult Humphrey Carpenter's *The Inklings*, Diana Glyer's *The Company They Keep*, and Colin Duriez's *Tolkien and C. S. Lewis: The Gift of Friendship*.

As the focus of this book is on Lewis's Chronicles of Narnia,

I will restrict myself in what follows to Narnia; however, before moving on, I would like to offer a least some brief guidance on Lewis's other works. For those wishing to move beyond Narnia to the wider Lewis corpus, the best place to start is The Complete C. S. Lewis Signature Series, which is published by HarperOne and that contains in a boxed set Lewis's seven finest Christian works: *Mere Christianity*, *The Screwtape Letters*, *The Great Divorce*, *Miracles*, *The Problem of Pain*, *A Grief Observed*, and *The Abolition of Man*. Interested readers should also purchase at some point *Reflections on the Psalms* and *The Four Loves*. In addition to his Chronicles, Lewis wrote a trilogy of science fiction novels that merit close reading. The three novels (*Out of the Silent Planet*, *Perelandra*, *That Hideous Strength*) are known collectively as The Space Trilogy and are available in a boxed set. He also wrote a mature and haunting novel titled *Till We Have Faces*. Of the many essay collections (all edited by Walter Hooper) the best are *God in the Dock* and *The Weight of Glory and Other Addresses*. Narnia lovers should also pick up *On Stories*. The most accessible of Lewis's many academic works are *A Preface to Paradise Lost* and *The Discarded Image* (which lays out the medieval conception of the universe).

RESOURCES ON NARNIA

The Chronicles of Narnia were first published from 1950–56, with one novel appearing each year in the following order: *The Lion, the Witch and the Wardrobe*, *Prince Caspian*, *The Voyage of the Dawn Treader*, *The Silver Chair*, *The Horse and His Boy*, *The Magician's Nephew*, and *The Last Battle*. Unfortunately, in what is, to my mind at least, the worst publishing decision since Gutenberg, the Chronicles are today exclusively published, not in the original order of publication, but in the order of Narnian chronology. Thus,

The Magician's Nephew (which details the creation of Narnia) has been moved to the number-one spot, while *The Horse and His Boy* (which takes place simultaneous with the last chapter of *The Lion, the Witch and the Wardrobe*) has been sandwiched in between *The Lion, the Witch and the Wardrobe* and *Prince Caspian*. It is true that Lewis, later in life, wrote in a letter to a child that it might be interesting to read the Chronicles in the order of Narnian chronology, but this hardly justifies the claim made on the copyright page of all new editions that Lewis "wanted" *The Magician's Nephew* "to be read as the first book in the series" and that the new ordering was the one that "Professor Lewis preferred." For one, if he had really wanted the new ordering, he would have had to do quite a lot of revising of both *The Magician's Nephew* and *The Lion, the Witch and the Wardrobe* to accommodate the change. For another, to read *The Magician's Nephew* first is to ruin the joy of discovery one feels as one learns the origins of things he has read about in the previous five Chronicles. To read *The Horse and His Boy* third is not only to break the continuity between *The Lion, the Witch and the Wardrobe* and *Prince Caspian*, but to shoo us off to Calormen just when we were starting to love Narnia. Finally, and perhaps most importantly, it is imperative that *The Lion, the Witch and the Wardrobe* be our doorway to Narnia: first, because it is written in such a way as to gradually draw us into Narnia (as *The Magician's Nephew* is not); second, because it is vital that we begin our journey with what might be called the Narnian Gospel—just as I would encourage a new Christian eager to read the Bible for the first time to begin not with Genesis but with one of the Gospels.

I could enumerate several more reasons, but I do not need to do so because Peter Schakel has already given us, in chapter 3 of *Imagination and the Arts in C. S. Lewis: Journeying to Narnia and Other*

Worlds (University of Missouri Press, 2002), a full and rich defense for reading the Chronicles in their original order of publication (this essay has also been anthologized in several other places, including a collection called *Narnia Beckons*, published in 2005 by BenBella books). Chapter 2 of *Imagination and the Arts* also merits a close reading, for it gives a very helpful publishing history of the Chronicles from their first appearance to the present day. Speaking of this, it should be noted that the Chronicles are today available in every possible shape and size, some of which have taken the original black-and-white drawings by Pauline Baynes and colorized them. There is even a one-volume hardcover edition of The Chronicles that contains all seven books under a single cover. Let your own aesthetic taste and pocketbook guide you in deciding which editions of the Chronicles to purchase.

Though the Narnia books are far less complex than *The Lord of the Rings*, they still, when taken cumulatively, encompass a great deal of names, places, and objects. For those who wish to sort these out, Paul Ford's *Companion to Narnia* (HarperSanFrancisco, 1980, with many reprints), offers a complete guide (organized alphabetically) to all seven novels. The *Companion* is fully cross-referenced, and one can literally spend hours "surfing" from one entry to the next. In his introduction, Ford also offers some of his own reasons for treating the Chronicles in their original order of publication.

In addition to Ford's encyclopedia, the Chronicles have inspired a number of books that attempt to unpack for the reader the Christian themes and ethical lessons that lie hidden beneath the surface of the narrative. The first major study to do so—one which garnered Lewis's stamp of approval—is Kathryn Lindskoog's *The Lion of Judah in Never-Never Land: The Theology of C. S.*

Lewis Expressed in His Fantasies for Children (Eerdmans, 1973). The book is a bit elementary, but it's a good place to start and is faithful to Lewis's intentions. Lindskoog later updated and expanded this work; it now appears under the title *Journey into Narnia*. A second book that goes a bit more in-depth is Peter Schakel's *Reading with the Heart: The Way into Narnia* (Eerdmans, 1979), a work that does a particularly fine job uncovering the archetypal patterns and images that underlie the Chronicles. The years leading up to the 2005 film release of *The Lion, the Witch and the Wardrobe* produced a number of Christian guides to the Chronicles — some of which can be a bit schematic, but which are helpful nonetheless, especially in teaching the Chronicles to children. These include: *A Family Guide to Narnia: Biblical Truths in C. S. Lewis's The Chronicles of Narnia* by Christin Ditchfield; *Into the Wardrobe: C. S. Lewis and the Narnia Chronicles* by David C. Downing; *Meeting God in The Lion, the Witch and the Wardrobe* by Sara McLaughlin; *A Field Guide to Narnia* by Colin Duriez; *A Reader's Guide Through the Wardrobe: Exploring C. S. Lewis's Classic Story* by Leland Ryken; and, *Aslan's Call: Finding Our Way to Narnia* by Mark Eddy Smith.

Some earlier, standard studies of Lewis's fiction include: Evan K. Gibson's *C. S. Lewis: Spinner of Tales* (Christian University Press, 1980); Thomas Howard's *The Achievements of C. S. Lewis: A Reading of His Fiction* (Harold Shaw, 1980; reissued in England in 1987 by Churchman Publishing, under the title: *C. S. Lewis: Man of Letters: A Reading of His Fiction*); and, Peter J. Schakel and Charles Huttar's *Word and Story in C. S. Lewis* (University of Missouri Press, 1991). For a book that looks at both Lewis and Tolkien, see Richard Purtill's *Lord of the Elves and Eldils: Fantasy and Philosophy in C. S. Lewis and J. R. R. Tolkien*. Brian Sibley's *The Land of Narnia: Brian Sibley Explores the World of C. S. Lewis* (HarperCollins, 1989) is a simple but wonderful book that can be enjoyed by children and their parents alike. It contains beautiful line drawings and watercolors by Pauline Baynes that are interspersed throughout the pages and margins of the text. This inexpensive book makes the perfect gift for an adolescent who has loved the Narnia books and wants to learn more about their maker and his world.

Finally, in 2008, lovers of Narnia received a great gift in the form of a new and exciting study of the Chronicles. Michael Ward's *Planet Narnia: The Seven Heavens in the Imagination of C. S. Lewis* (Oxford University Press) offers a brilliant and fresh reading of the Chronicles that argues that Lewis keyed each of the seven novels to the seven medieval "planets": Moon (*The Silver Chair*), Mercury (*The Horse and His Boy*), Venus (*The Magician's Nephew*), Sun (*The Voyage of the Dawn Treader*), Mars (*Prince Caspian*), Jupiter (*The Lion, the Witch and the Wardrobe*), and Saturn (*The Last Battle*). Ward argues convincingly for numerous links between the novels and the influences of each of the planets. Lewis was a great lover of the medieval cosmological model, a model which he lays out in all its glory in his academic work (especially *The Discarded Image*), which appears often in his early poetry (especially "The Planets," from which Ward quotes at length and on which he bases much of his argument), and which plays a central role in his Space Trilogy (for which Ward also offers a number of fresh interpretations). Those who think they have traced every allusion in the Chronicles and mined it for its full freight of meaning will find, after reading *Planet Narnia*, that there are still countless treasures to be excavated! This is not only the best book on Narnia in ten years, it is one of the four or five best books ever written on Lewis and his rich and diverse body of work.

THE CHRONICLES IN RADIO, TV, AND FILM

The first four books of the Chronicles of Narnia have been filmed (in live action) by the BBC as part of the WonderWorks Series (1988). The series consists of three three-hour segments. Part I is devoted entirely to *The Lion, the Witch and the Wardrobe*; Part II devotes its first hour to *Prince Caspian* and the latter two to *The Voyage of the Dawn Treader*; Part III retells *The Silver Chair*. The films are enchanting, if a bit stiff and chatty at times, and will delight children. They are faithful to the books and do the stories justice. They also improve as they go along, wonderfully realizing Reepicheep and finding fine actors to play King Caspian and Puddleglum. *The Lion, the Witch and the Wardrobe* has also been made into a delightful, Emmy Award–winning animated film that I find more compelling than the live-action BBC version. In a mere 95 minutes it captures the full flavor of the book. Best of all, Focus on the Family's Radio Theater has turned all seven Chronicles into excellent radio plays that are faithful to the novels and done with great style. They are all introduced by Douglas Gresham (Lewis's stepson), and they include the voices of Paul Scofield as the narrator and David Suchet as Aslan. When my family is not listening to the BBC radio plays of *The Lord of the Rings*, we listen to these masterful versions of the Chronicles. They are ideal for long car trips and are guaranteed to captivate adults and children alike. The Chronicles are also available in unabridged audio book format, read by such great British actors as Kenneth Branagh, Patrick Stewart, Michael York, and Derek Jacobi (Harper Audio).

Finally, in December of 2005, *The Lion, the Witch and the Wardrobe* was made into a wonderful motion picture, produced by Walden Media and Disney and directed by Andrew Adamson. Shot in New Zealand, like the LOTR, the film boasts cutting-edge special effects by WETA and brilliantly realizes the characters and landscapes of Narnia. The movie is faithful to the plot and gives us both battles and a "crucifixion" scene that are thrilling and frightening while yet being appropriate for small children to watch (the film is PG, whereas the LOTR films are PG-13). In several ways, one could argue, the movie even improves on the novel: 1) it draws richer connections between the World War II setting of the novel and the Narnian war being waged between Aslan and the White Witch; 2) it develops the relationships between the four Pevensie children and allows us to watch as they grow from normal kids into heroes; 3) it expands on the character of Mr. Tumnus and powerfully contrasts Tumnus with Edmund. However, the film has one major flaw: it both downplays and diminishes the character of Aslan. It does so in two ways. First, it greatly expands the role of the children at the expense of Aslan, making it seem as if Aslan is there to assist the children rather than vice versa. Second, and more disturbing, Aslan is robbed of most of his numinous power. The film Aslan simply does not evoke in the viewer the proper awe, respect, and fear. Still, the film is excellent and is essential viewing for all lovers of Narnia.

In May of 2008, a darker, yet still family friendly film version of *Prince Caspian* was released that was superior to the first film in terms of plotting, characterization, direction, cinematography, music, and special effects, but which was less faithful to the novel and its Christian message. In keeping with Peter Jackson's LOTR films, *Prince Caspian* extends and even adds battle scenes: 1) it gives us a richly cinematic, adrenaline-pumping battle of brains and brawn outside Aslan's How; 2) it adds a new scene, replete with heroism, fear, confusion, and self-sacrifice, in which Caspian and Peter mount a failed raid on Miraz's castle. The failure of the raid is due to two major character changes made in the film: 1) Caspian impulsively seeks out the bedchamber of his uncle, whom he plans to kill in retribution for Miraz's murder of his father; 2) scores of Narnians die needlessly because Peter allows pride, stubbornness, and a refusal to accept that he does not have everything under control to delay fatally his call to retreat. Caspian's attempt to kill his uncle occurs because the film ages Caspian about five years, giving him a more adult, more self-conscious need to exercise his own authority and to avenge his father. Peter's pride comes from something Lewis does not consider in his novel—what it must have been like for the Pevensies to return to England as children after having spent many years as adult rulers of Narnia. In Peter's case, it has made him edgy, impatient, and desperate to prove his valor and maturity. The film also prepares us for Susan's later loss of status as a Narnian queen (something that occurs in *The Last Battle* but which Lewis was unaware of when he wrote *Prince Caspian*) in two ways: 1) she's less happy than Lucy to be in Narnia because she had just gotten used to our world; 2) she has a poignant teenage crush on Caspian that seems to foreshadow the comment made in *The Last Battle* that Susan prefers "nylons and lipstick and invitations" to talking about Narnia. As in the film version of *The Lion, the Witch and the Wardrobe*, these changes to the children make for richer characterization and represent, arguably, an improvement on the novel.

Unfortunately, though the film tightens up Lewis's rather loose plotting, offers us an excellent set piece in Aslan's How, develops the interplay between Miraz and his advisors, provides magical transitions between Narnia and our world, and wonderfully incarnates Reepicheep, Trufflehunter, and an imposing river god, it misses those aspects of the novel where Lewis's Christian message is most strong. First, the film muffles the subtle distinctions that Lewis draws between Trumpkin and Nikabrik: though, in the beginning, both are crotchety "secular humanists" who consider Aslan and the four children to be fairy tales, Lewis shows how the former grows into a faithful servant of Aslan while the latter goes sour inside and dies attempting to bring back the White Witch. Second, the film misunderstands (whether intentionally or not) that the Telmarines are not just totalitarians; they embody post-Christian Europe. They have not just driven the Narnians underground but have eradicated their memory. They paint old Narnia as dark and medieval, engulfed by ignorance and superstition, yet they secretly fear those "superstitions." As for the Old Narnians who follow Caspian, they are not just a rebel army but a persecuted remnant "church" desperately holding on to their faith in a risen redeemer-king.

Third, the film leaves out entirely a vital episode in the novel. While the boys (Peter, Edmund, and Caspian) are defeating the physical weapons of Miraz, the girls (Susan and Lucy) ride atop Aslan, who, with the help of Bacchus and his divine madness, charges through the Narnian countryside freeing the hearts and spirits of his people from Telmarine censorship and repression. Had the filmmakers chosen to maintain this episode, they could have built up some powerful parallel action that they could then have climaxed at the bridge of Beruna; instead, they leave out this scene altogether, thus giving Aslan very little to do. Finally, this film, like the previous one, robs Aslan of his numinous power. Though it retains most of Aslan's key lines, it tends to tick them off without conviction. The scenes with Aslan are rushed and ultimately carry little power. Still, the film, *as* a film, is quite good and all true Narnians should give it several viewings.

In December of 2010 an entertaining film version of Lewis's third Chronicle, *The Voyage of the Dawn Treader*, arrived in theaters. Although *Dawn Treader* is the most epic of the novels, it is also the most episodic. It is therefore not surprising that the film rearranges the major episodes of the book and inserts a narrative device — involving seven magic swords — to give unity and purpose to its discrete adventures. The film provides us with swashbuckling sword fights, well-chosen island locales, sweeping cinematography, magical special effects, an excellent CGI dragon and sea serpent, and a first-rate ship. It is also anchored firmly within a good-versus-evil matrix that prevents it from drifting downward into ethical relativism or postmodern inclusivism. And it maintains the all-important final scene in which Aslan clearly presents himself to the children as the Christ of Narnia.

As in the earlier two films, the characters of the children are well developed and given a psychological richness absent from the novel. Caspian, desperate to live up to the high reputation of his late father, struggles throughout the film with his inadequacies as successor. Edmund, meanwhile, has never forgotten the White Witch's promise to make him High King; he despises the Witch, yet a part of him is as desperate as Caspian to prove his worth and his courage. In an added scene that does not appear in the novel, the two young men meet Father and Witch and are forced to choose the path of good or evil.

True to the novel, the film spends more time developing Lucy's struggles and growth than those of her brother. While flipping through the Magician's Book, Lucy comes upon a spell that will make her as pretty as Susan. As in the novel, Aslan prevents her from reading the spell, but the film adds a new twist: Lucy rips the spell out of the book and, back on board the Dawn Treader, reads it out loud. In a lovely use of film magic, Lucy transforms into Susan and walks through a mirror into a gleamingly photographed World War II dance. Lucy is elated, until she realizes that by getting her wish to be Susan, she (Lucy) no longer exists, and neither she nor her siblings know about Narnia. Realizing the consequences of getting her wish, Lucy rejects this alternate reality and returns to the ship; whereupon, Aslan appears in the mirror to tell her that she must accept herself for who and what she is.

It is a sweet message, and a very American one, but it does a disservice to the deeper ethical lessons taught by Lewis. In the novel, Lucy, upset that Aslan prevented her from saying the beautifying spell, impulsively speaks a different spell that allows her to eavesdrop on a friend back in England who, prodded by a bully, says something negative about Lucy. In a huff, Lucy curses the little traitor. Later, when Aslan assures her that her friend loves her, Lucy replies that she can never forget what she heard . . . to which Aslan replies that she never will! Lewis's Lucy must understand that her bad choices have lasting consequences, that she will never know what her friendship with the girl would have been like had she not spoken the spell.

As for Eustace, the film fully realizes the many dimensions of his character, allowing the audience to be annoyed by him without ever quite hating him. It also carefully modulates and develops the relationship between the spoiled and cowardly Eustace and the bold and chivalrous Reepicheep. Reepicheep's attempts to teach Eustace the rudiments of good behavior are both funny and touching, and the screen springs to life when Reepicheep challenges Eustace to an exciting and marvelously choreographed duel. Unfortunately, the film cuts back too severely on the dragoning and un-dragoning of Eustace, stripping it of most of its spiritual meaning. The film consistently eliminates or downplays those moments in the novel when Eustace, Lucy, and Edmund realize their ultimate inadequacy to save themselves and turn to Aslan for aid. It also, sadly, leaves out the vital character of Ramandu the magician and most of the final four chapters of the book when the Dawn Treader journeys into greater and greater light.

Still, despite leaving out much of what makes *The Voyage of the Dawn Treader* a book to treasure and contemplate, the film nevertheless remains faithful to the adventures and the characters that go on them. It offers a journey well worth taking and has the power to transform even the most calculating, left-brained, unimaginative child into a sailor of the high seas.

POSTSCRIPT

If you are ever in the vicinity of Wheaton College (located in Wheaton, Illinois, a suburb of Chicago), make sure to visit the Marion E. Wade Collection, which not only houses the best collection of Lewis's original manuscripts, letters, and papers, but features an extensive collection as well of the work of the other members of the Inklings (including J. R. R. Tolkien). It also contains the original wardrobe from Lewis's boyhood home.

ACKNOWLEDGMENTS

I have dedicated this book to our two children, Alexander and Anastasia (Stacey), not only because they are an excellent son and daughter but because they have succeeded so beautifully in taking to heart something I have tried to teach them since they were little:

The world is full of magic: you just need eyes to see it and ears to hear it.

Indeed, they have so taken this proverb to heart that they have returned the favor by helping me to see again the wonders of Narnia, Middle-earth, and our own no-less wondrous world. May the Lord of the Road bless you both as you go, Frodo-like and Reepicheep-like, on your own personal journeys and adventures.

There are another group of children (well, young adults) who have helped to keep my eyes and ears sharp over the last two decades. I speak, of course, of my college students—not only those who major in English and take my classes, but especially those who attend a weekly Bible study that my wife and I hold at our home. In a book I published in 2003 (*Lewis Agonistes*), I highlighted twenty students who have exerted a strong influence on me. I would like now to highlight a second batch of twenty-one who, between the spring of 2006 and the spring of 2010, have grown along with me and burned the midnight oil as we sang and talked and prayed late into the night—most of them even took one or both of my classes on Narnia and Middle-earth. I could easily name thirty or forty, but I will confine myself to twenty-one who have been particularly constant: Laurianne Balkum, Jennifer Barton, Rebecca Barton, Kristen Behne, Beth Bottom, Gary Cook, Adrienne Duhe, Aleeza Flores, James Hernandez, Josh Jones, Jacqueline Klein, Emily Klotz, Richard Lawson, Adriana Marachlian, David Mathew, Sandra Mathoslah, Terrace Menon, Angela Merkle, Angela Petry, Simeon Snow, and John Valentine.

In *Lewis Agonistes* I also acknowledged a number of administrators who have supported and encouraged my work over the years. I would like here to thank five more recent Houston Baptist University leaders whose advocacy of my work has been invaluable: President Robert Sloan, Provost Paul Bonicelli, Associate Provost Robert Stacey, Dean Diane Lovell, and Dean David Capes. Due in great part to their advocacy, HBU awarded me, in 2009, the Robert H. Ray Chair in Humanities and the title of Scholar-in-Residence, awards that have given me the necessary time and opportunity to bring this book to completion. In addition, they helped pave the way for me to teach the freshman classical Christian curriculum for HBU's Honors College, a position that has inspired me in a multitude of ways, drawing me closer both to my students and to the Great Books of the Western Canon.

Finally to the baker's dozen of friends that I thanked in *Lewis Agonistes* I would like to add a much longer list of friends who have been instrumental to my growth as an author and public speaker: Rick Baldwin, Matt Boyleston, Connie Charalampos, Nick Checkles, Lawrence Clark, George Dehan, Art Dimopoulos, Ben Domenech, Jerry Eisley, Miguel Estrada, Betty Feehan, Tom Fox, Jim Freeman, Steve Garfinkel, Anne Graves, Wayne Green, Stan Guthrie, Joel Heck, Rick Hooten, John Hughson, Tom Kirkpatrick, Kevin Koecher, Anthony Kouzounis, Eric Ladau, Bill Lederer, Bill Martin, Jay McCaslin, Mitti Meyers, David Mills, Margaret Mims, Henry Nuss, Joseph Pearce, Steve Rummelsburg (and his lovely wife and daughters), George Saxon, Joel Scandrett, Scott Susong, Rita Tauer, Justin Taylor, Bob Trexler, Troy Wathen, Alida Webb, Sue Wendling, Linda Woodward, and Tom Woodward.

INDEX